SOCIAL ISSUES, JUSTICE AND STATUS

FOOD INSECURITY IN U.S. HOUSEHOLDS WITH CHILDREN

TRENDS AND ANALYSIS

SOCIAL ISSUES, JUSTICE AND STATUS

Additional books in this series can be found on Nova's website under the Series tab.

Additional e-books in this series can be found on Nova's website under the e-book tab.

NUTRITION AND DIET RESEARCH PROGRESS

Additional books in this series can be found on Nova's website under the Series tab.

Additional e-books in this series can be found on Nova's website under the e-book tab.

SOCIAL ISSUES, JUSTICE AND STATUS

FOOD INSECURITY IN U.S. HOUSEHOLDS WITH CHILDREN

TRENDS AND ANALYSIS

DUSTIN C. BERTRAM
EDITOR

NOVINKA

New York

For permission to use material from this book please contact us:
Telephone 631-231-7269; Fax 631-231-8175
Web Site: http://www.novapublishers.com

Additional color graphics may be available in the e-book version of this book.

Library of Congress Cataloging-in-Publication Data

ISBN: 978-1-62948-015-2

Published by Nova Science Publishers, Inc. †New York

CONTENTS

PREFACE

Most U.S. households with children have consistent, dependable access to adequate food for active, healthy living for both adults and children—they are food secure. However, 21 percent of households with children were food insecure at times during the year in 2011, and in some of those households, children as well as adults were food insecure. The U.S. Department of Agriculture (USDA) monitors the extent and severity of food insecurity in U.S. households through an annual, nationally representative survey, with special attention to households with children. Food security is especially important for children because their nutrition affects not only their current health, but also their physical, mental, and social development—and thus their future health and well-being. Previous studies suggest that children living in food-insecure households face elevated risks of many problematic health and development outcomes, compared with children in otherwise similar food-secure households. USDA's domestic food and nutrition assistance programs improve children's food security by providing low-income households with access to a healthful diet and nutrition education. Knowledge about the extent of food insecurity in households with children and the household characteristics associated with food insecurity contributes to the effective operation of these and other programs that support the well-being of children. This book describes the extent and severity of food insecurity in households with children in 2011, food security trends since 1999, and characteristics of households affected by food insecurity in 2010 and 2011.

Chapter 1 – An estimated 79 percent of households with children were food secure throughout the year in 2011, meaning that all the household members had consistent access to adequate food for active, healthy lives. The remainder (nearly 21 percent) were food insecure at some time during the year, including 10 percent in which children were food insecure and 1 percent in which one or more children experienced very low food security—the most severe food-insecure condition measured by USDA. In this latter 1 percent of households, caregivers reported that children were hungry, skipped a meal, or did not eat for a whole day because there was not enough money for food. A range of studies suggest that children in food-insecure households face higher risks of problematic health and development outcomes than children in otherwise similar food-secure households. The present study shows that in 2010-11, 75 percent of households with food-insecure children had one or more adults in the labor force, including 60 percent with a full-time worker. More than half of households with food-insecure children included an adult with education beyond high school, including 15 percent with an adult who held a 4-year college degree. Federal food and nutrition assistance programs provided benefits to 84 percent of low-income food-insecure households with children in 2010-11.

Chapter 2 – Federally supported child nutrition programs and initiatives, along with the Special Supplemental Nutrition Program for Women, Infants, and Children (the WIC program) reach more than 40 million children and some 2 million lower-income pregnant/post-partum women. In FY2007, federal spending on these programs totaled over $19 billion.

The basic goals of federal child nutrition programs are to improve children's nutrition, increase lower-income children's access to nutritious meals and snacks, and help support the agricultural economy. Child nutrition programs are "entitlements." Federal cash funding and commodity support is "guaranteed" to schools and other providers based on the number of meals/snacks served, who is served (e.g., free meals for poor children get higher subsidies), and legislatively established (and inflation-indexed) per-meal subsidy rates. On the other hand, the WIC program is a "discretionary" grant program where specific annual appropriations to pay for benefits and nutrition services and administration are distributed by formula.

In addition to the WIC program (and its ancillary farmers' market program), the child nutrition programs covered in this report include the School Lunch and Breakfast programs (providing federal subsidies for meals served in schools), day-care, summer and other outside-of-school programs assisting sponsors in providing meals/snacks, and payments to states covering administrative oversight costs, expenses for a Fresh Fruit and Vegetable program, the Special Milk program, and various support activities (e.g., various administrative oversight and nutrition education activities).

The underlying laws covering child nutrition and WIC programs were last reauthorized in 2004 in the Child Nutrition and WIC Reauthorization Act (P.L. 108-265). The next reauthorization is scheduled for 2009. The Administration's FY2010 budget calls for increased funding of approximately $1 billion a year for child nutrition programs (for "program reforms aimed at improving program access, enhancing the nutritional quality of school meals, expanding nutrition research and evaluation, and improving program oversight").

In: Food Insecurity in U.S. Households ... ISBN: 978-1-62948-015-2
Editor: Dustin C. Bertram

Chapter 1

FOOD INSECURITY IN HOUSEHOLDS WITH CHILDREN: PREVALENCE, SEVERITY, AND HOUSEHOLD CHARACTERISTICS, 2010-11*

Alisha Coleman-Jensen, William McFall and Mark Nord

ABSTRACT

An estimated 79 percent of households with children were food secure throughout the year in 2011, meaning that all the household members had consistent access to adequate food for active, healthy lives. The remainder (nearly 21 percent) were food insecure at some time during the year, including 10 percent in which children were food insecure and 1 percent in which one or more children experienced very low food security—the most severe food-insecure condition measured by USDA. In this latter 1 percent of households, caregivers reported that children were hungry, skipped a meal, or did not eat for a whole day because there was not enough money for food. A range of studies suggest that children in food-insecure households face higher risks of problematic health and development outcomes than children in otherwise similar food-secure households. The present study shows that in 2010-11, 75 percent of households with food-insecure children had one or more adults in the labor force, including 60 percent with a full-time worker. More than half of households with food-insecure children included an adult

* This is an edited, reformatted and augmented version of Economic Research Service, Economic Information Bulletin Number 113, dated May 2013.

with education beyond high school, including 15 percent with an adult who held a 4-year college degree. Federal food and nutrition assistance programs provided benefits to 84 percent of low-income food-insecure households with children in 2010-11.

SUMMARY

What Is the Issue?

Most U.S. households with children have consistent, dependable access to adequate food for active, healthy living for both adults and children—they are food secure. However, 21 percent of households with children were food insecure at times during the year in 2011, and in some of those households, children as well as adults were food insecure. The U.S. Department of Agriculture (USDA) monitors the extent and severity of food insecurity in U.S. households through an annual, nationally representative survey, with special attention to households with children.

Food security is especially important for children because their nutrition affects not only their current health, but also their physical, mental, and social development—and thus their future health and well-being. Previous studies suggest that children living in food-insecure households face elevated risks of many problematic health and development outcomes, compared with children in otherwise similar food-secure households. USDA's domestic food and nutrition assistance programs improve children's food security by providing low-income households with access to a healthful diet and nutrition education. Knowledge about the extent of food insecurity in households with children and the household characteristics associated with food insecurity contributes to the effective operation of these and other programs that support the well-being of children. This report describes the extent and severity of food insecurity in households with children in 2011, food security trends since 1999, and characteristics of households affected by food insecurity in 2010 and 2011. A previous ERS report described the characteristics of food-insecure households with children as of 2007.

What Did the Study Find?

The ERS report *Household Food Security in the United States in 2011* (September 2012) indicated that 79 percent of households with children were food secure throughout the year, meaning they had consistent access to adequate food for active, healthy lives for all household members. The remaining nearly 21 percent of households with children were food insecure at some time during the year. In about half of those households, only adults were food insecure, but in 10 percent of all households with children, one or more of the children also were food insecure at some time during the year. In 1.0 percent of households with children, one or more child experienced the most severe food-insecure condition monitored by USDA—very low food security. In households with very low food security among children, caregivers had reported that children were hungry, skipped a meal, or did not eat for a whole day because there was not enough money for food.

This study, focusing on households with children age 0-17, averaged 2 years of data (2010-11) and found that in households headed by an unemployed adult, the prevalence of food insecurity among children was three and a half times as high as in households headed by one or more adult employed full-time. However, three-quarters of households with food-insecure children had one or more adult in the labor force, either full time (60 percent) or part time (15 percent).

- For households headed by an adult with less than a high school diploma, the prevalence of food insecurity among children was six and a half times as high as for households headed by an adult with at least a 4-year college degree.
- Children were food insecure in about 20 percent of households that included an adult who was out of the labor force because of disability, compared with about 9 percent of households in which no working-age adult had a disability.
- Federal food and nutrition assistance programs provided benefits to 84 percent of low-income households with food-insecure children (low-income households are those with incomes below 185 percent of the Federal poverty line).
- Children in about 70 percent of low-income households with food-insecure children received free or reduced-price school meals in 2010-11, about 42 percent of low-income households with food-insecure children received Supplemental Nutrition Assistance Program

(SNAP) benefits, and about 25 percent received Special Supplemental Nutrition Program for Women, Infants, and Children (WIC) benefits. Many households received assistance from multiple programs, although about 31 percent reported receiving only free or reduced-price school meals.

- Low-income households not receiving assistance from any of the programs were less likely to be food insecure (12 percent) than those that did receive assistance (approximately 23-30 percent, depending on the mix of programs). This difference suggests that low-income households with greater food security are less likely to choose to participate in food assistance programs.
- Food insecurity among children was more likely for households that had left SNAP during the previous year than for those currently receiving benefits. This finding suggests that some households left the program even though their economic resources were not yet adequate to meet their food needs.

How Was the Study Conducted?

Data for the study came from annual food security surveys sponsored by USDA's Economic Research Service and conducted by the Department of Commerce's U.S. Census Bureau as supplements to the monthly Current Population Survey. The survey respondents were representative samples of the U.S. civilian noninstitutionalized population and included 13,000-18,000 households with children each year. The food security survey asked one adult respondent in each household a series of questions about experiences and behaviors that indicate food insecurity. The food security status of the household was assessed based on the number of food-insecure conditions reported (such as being unable to afford balanced meals, cutting the size of meals because there was too little money for food, or being hungry because there was too little money for food). The food security status of children in the household was assessed by responses to a subset of questions about the conditions and experiences of children in the household. Survey respondents also reported whether, and to what extent, they used food and nutrition assistance programs. Peer-reviewed studies on those topics by other researchers were reviewed and summarized to provide information on how children's health and development may be affected by food insecurity.

INTRODUCTION

Food security—access at all times to enough food for an active, healthy life— provides an important foundation for good nutrition and health. Food security is especially important for children because the nutritional content of their diets affects not only their current health, but also their physical, mental, and social development—and thus, their future health and well-being.

USDA provides annual statistics on the food security of U.S. households, including summary statistics on households with children by demographic characteristics and income (Coleman-Jensen et al., 2012). This report gives additional detailed information on the food security of households with children in 2010-11 and presents a breakdown by household characteristics, such as the employment, education, and disability status of adults in the household.

Food security statistics are also provided for households with children using various Federal food and nutrition assistance programs. Our findings update those from a previous report on food insecurity in households with children as of 2007 (Nord, 2009). Differences across groups and changes from the previous report are mentioned in the text only if they are statistically significant at the 90-percent confidence level. All household statistics in this report refer to households with children age 0-17.

In fiscal year (FY) 2011, USDA spent about $103.8 billion on domestic food and nutrition assistance programs to ensure access to nutritious, healthful diets for all Americans (Oliveira, 2013). Children make up the largest share of the beneficiaries of those programs.

Almost half of the beneficiaries of the largest program—the Supplemental Nutrition Assistance Program (SNAP, formerly called the Food Stamp Program)—are children younger than age 18. The second and third largest programs—the National School Lunch Program (NSLP) and the Special Supplemental Nutrition Program for Women, Infants, and Children (WIC)—focus primarily on children. Understanding the extent of food insecurity in households with children and characteristics associated with food insecurity contributes to the effective operation of these and other programs that support the well-being of children.

Food Security and Insecurity: Concepts and 2011 National Statistics

Food insecurity—the lack of consistent access to adequate food—is an economic and social condition that may result in hunger (a physiological condition) if it is severe or prolonged. USDA differentiates food-insecure households by the severity of food insecurity they have experienced (see box, "About the Data," p. 4). Food insecurity in households with children is differentiated further by whether it affects only adults or also affects children and by the severity of food insecurity among the children.

In 2011, 85.1 percent of all U.S. households were *food secure* throughout the year. The remaining 14.9 percent of all households (17.9 million households) were *food insecure* at some time during the year. The prevalence of food insecurity was lower for households with no children under age 18 than for households with children. In 2011, 12.2 percent of households with no children under age 18 (9.9 million households) were *food insecure* at some time during the year (Coleman-Jensen et al., 2012).

In 2011, 79.4 percent of households with children (30.8 million households) were *food secure* throughout the year (fig. 1). The remaining 20.6 percent of households with children (8.0 million households) were *food insecure* at some time during the year.

Parents often are able to maintain normal or near-normal diets and meal patterns for their children, even when the parents themselves are food insecure. In about half of food-insecure households with children in 2011, only adults were food insecure; in the rest, children were also food insecure. Thus, in 10 percent of all households with children (3.9 million households), children were sometimes food insecure. USDA refers to these households as having *food insecurity among children*.

In 1.0 percent of households with children (374,000 households), food insecurity among children was so severe that caregivers reported that children were hungry, skipped a meal, or did not eat for a whole day because there was not enough money for food. USDA describes these households as having *very low food security* among children.

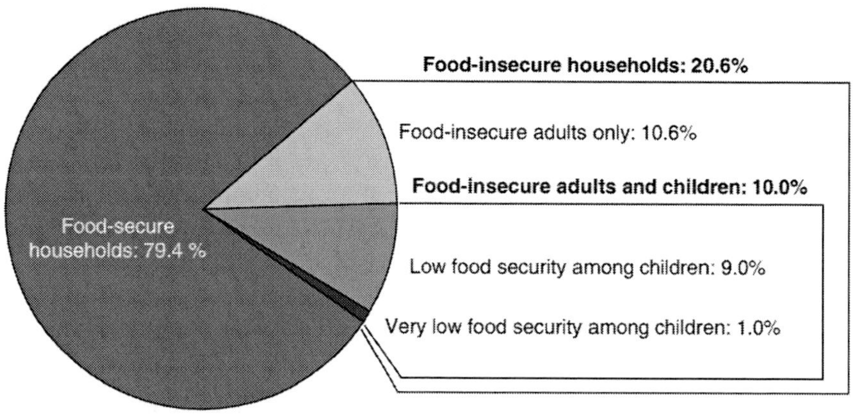

Source: USDA, Economic Research Service calculations based on data from the December 2011 Current Population Survey Food Security Supplement.

Figure 1. Food security status of households with children, 2011

Adults, children, or both were food insecure at some time during the year in 20.6 percent of households with children. In 10.0 percent of households with children, children were food insecure (with either low or very low food security) at some time during the year.

About the Data

Data for this study came from annual food security surveys sponsored by USDA and conducted by the U.S. Census Bureau from 1999 to 2011 as supplements to the monthly Current Population Survey (CPS). The surveys were of representative samples of the U.S. civilian population and included between 13,000 and 18,000 households with children each year. The survey was conducted both by telephone and in person so that households with no telephone would not be underrepresented. The food security survey asked one adult respondent in each household a series of questions about experiences and behaviors that indicate food insecurity. The food security status of the household was assessed based on the number of food-insecure conditions reported (such as being unable to afford balanced meals, cutting the size of meals because there was too little money for food, or being hungry because there was too little money for food). The food security questions from the survey are presented in the box on page 6.

The food security status of children in the household was assessed by responses to a subset of questions about the conditions and experiences of children. Survey respondents also reported whether they had used various Federal food and nutrition assistance programs.

Household characteristics (other than food security and receipt of food and nutrition assistance) were calculated from data collected in the labor force section of the CPS. The core CPS collects data on household composition, household income, demographic information for each household member, disability status, and employment information for all persons age 15 and older.

Weighting factors were calculated by the U.S. Census Bureau so that, when properly weighted, responses to the food security questions were representative at State and national levels. All statistics in this report were calculated by applying the appropriate weights to responses of the surveyed households to obtain nationally representative prevalence estimates.

Limitations of the Data

Some limitations to the data exist that may affect estimates of food insecurity. The CPS selects households to interview from a list of addresses and does not include homeless individuals or families. The omission of homeless persons may bias food insecurity and very low food security estimates downward. With regard to food insecurity among children, in particular, parents or caregivers may be embarrassed or afraid to report that their children are not getting enough to eat, so food insecurity among children may be underreported. Additionally, parents may believe that they have protected their children from experiencing food insecurity, but older children may have reduced their own food intake in response to household food insecurity without their parents' knowledge. The extent of bias related to homelessness and misreports of children's food insecurity is unknown.

FOOD-INSECURE HOUSEHOLDS WITH CHILDREN: SEVERITY OF FOOD INSECURITY

The severity of food access problems in each category of food insecurity can be gauged by the specific conditions reported by households in that category. The food security status of households with children is assessed by adult responses to a series of 18 questions about conditions and behaviors that typically occur in households when they have difficulty meeting their food needs (see box, "Questions Used To Assess the Food Security of Households in USDA's Annual Food Security Survey," p. 6). Households reporting three or more indicators of food insecurity in response to any of the 18 questions are classified as food insecure. In many of these households, only adults are food insecure.

The food security status of children is assessed by responses of an adult in the household to the eight questions about food-related conditions among children (questions 11-18; see box, "Questions Used To Assess the Food Security of Households in USDA's Annual Food Security Survey," p. 6). Households that report two or more food-insecure conditions among children are classified as having *food insecurity among children.* These households are classified further as having *low* or *very low food security among children.* Households reporting two to four conditions that indicate food insecurity among children are classified as having *low food security among children.*[1] Those reporting five or more conditions are classified as having *very low food security among children.* Figure 2 depicts the share of households in each food-insecure category that reported each of the eight indicators of food insecurity among children in the 2010 and 2011 food security surveys. (Two years of data were combined to provide more stable and reliable estimates.)

Food Insecurity among Adults Only

Households with food insecurity among adults only are classified as food insecure, but report no food-insecure conditions among children or only one such condition. (Two or more indicators are required to classify the household as having food insecurity among children.) About 42 percent of households with food insecurity only among adults reported no indicators of food insecurity among children. The remaining households in this category (58 percent) reported one indicator of food insecurity among children. The majority of those reporting one indicator reported the least severe one (i.e., that they had relied on a few kinds of low-cost foods to feed the children because they were running out of money to buy food).

Questions Used To Assess the Food Security of Households in USDA's Annual Food Security Survey

1. "We worried whether our food would run out before we got money to buy more." Was that often, sometimes, or never true for you in the last 12 months?
2. "The food that we bought just didn't last and we didn't have money to get more." Was that often, sometimes, or never true for you in the last 12 months?
3. "We couldn't afford to eat balanced meals." Was that often, sometimes, or never true for you in the last 12 months?
4. In the last 12 months, did you or other adults in the household ever cut the size of your meals or skip meals because there wasn't enough money for food? (Yes/No)
5. (If yes to question 4) How often did this happen—almost every month, some months but not every month, or in only 1 or 2 months?
6. In the last 12 months, did you ever eat less than you felt you should because there wasn't enough money for food? (Yes/No)
7. In the last 12 months, were you ever hungry, but didn't eat, because there wasn't enough money for food? (Yes/No)
8. In the last 12 months, did you lose weight because there wasn't enough money for food? (Yes/No)
9. In the last 12 months, did you or other adults in your household ever not eat for a whole day because there wasn't enough money for food? (Yes/No)
10. (If yes to question 9) How often did this happen—almost every month, some months but not every month, or in only 1 or 2 months?

(Questions 11-18 were asked only if the household included children ages 0-17)

11. "We relied on only a few kinds of low-cost food to feed our children because we were running out of money to buy food." Was that often, sometimes, or never true for you in the last 12 months?
12. "We couldn't feed our children a balanced meal, because we couldn't afford that." Was that often, sometimes, or never true for you in the last 12 months?

13. "The children were not eating enough because we just couldn't afford enough food." Was that often, sometimes, or never true for you in the last 12 months?
14. In the last 12 months, did you ever cut the size of any of the children's meals because there wasn't enough money for food? (Yes/No)
15. In the last 12 months, were the children ever hungry but you just couldn't afford more food? (Yes/No)
16. In the last 12 months, did any of the children ever skip a meal because there wasn't enough money for food? (Yes/ No)
17. (If yes to question 16) How often did this happen—almost every month, some months but not every month, or in only 1 or 2 months?
18. In the last 12 months, did any of the children ever not eat for a whole day because there wasn't enough money for food? (Yes/No)

Coding of Responses

Questions 1-3 and 11-13 are coded as affirmative (i.e., possibly indicating food insecurity) if the response is "often" or "sometimes." Questions 5, 10, and 17 are coded as affirmative if the response is "almost every month" or "some months but not every month." The remaining questions are coded as affirmative if the response is "yes."

Assessing Food Security Status

Households are classified as food insecure if they report three or more indications of food insecurity in response to the entire set of 18 questions.

The food security status of children in the household is assessed by responses to the child-referenced questions (questions 11-18). Households reporting two or more of these conditions are classified as having food insecurity among children. Households reporting five or more are classified as having very low food security among children.

Low Food Security among Children

Households with low (but not very low) food security among children mainly reported reductions in the quality and variety of children's meals. About half of these households reported some reduction in the amount of food children ate, but only 5 percent reported more than a single indicator of reduced food intake.

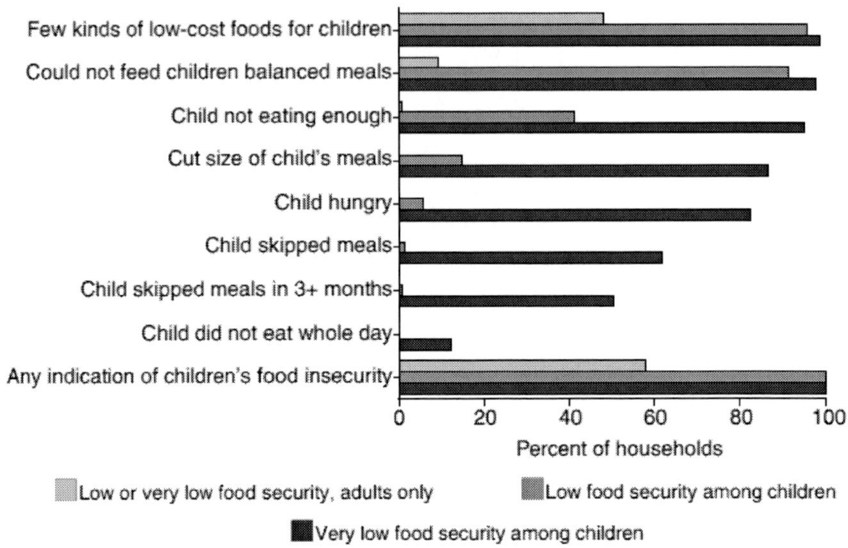

Note: See the box on the food security survey questions for complete wording of the questions.

Source: USDA, Economic Research Service calculations based on Current Population Survey Food Security Supplement data.

Figure 2. Reported conditions in food-insecure households with children, by food security status, 2010-11 average.

Very Low Food Security among Children

Very low food security among children is a severe range of food insecurity identified by caregivers who report five or more food-insecure conditions among children. Taken together, these reports indicate that children are not getting enough to eat. Households with very low food security among children all reported multiple indicators of reduced food intake. Almost 83 percent reported that at some time during the year a child had been hungry, but the household just could not afford more food (and also reported four other indicators of food-insecure conditions among children). Those households that did not report that a child had been hungry reported that either a child had skipped a meal or had not eaten for a whole day because there was not enough money for food.

FOOD INSECURITY AND CHILDHOOD HUNGER

Statistics on food insecurity among children provide important information about the social and economic context in which childhood hunger may occur, but they do not indicate directly the extent of hunger. Although hunger is related to food insecurity, it is a different phenomenon. Food insecurity is a household-level economic and social condition of limited access to food, while hunger is an individual-level physiological condition that may result from food insecurity (National Research Council, 2006). Thus, hunger is a potential, although not inevitable, outcome of food insecurity.

Specific information about the incidence of hunger would be of considerable interest to advocates, policymakers, and researchers and might be of value for policy and program design. USDA's nutrition assistance programs are intended, in part, to prevent or alleviate hunger. But providing precise and useful statistics about hunger has been hampered by lack of a consistent definition of the word and a validated method for measuring it. "Hunger" is variously understood to refer to conditions across a broad range of severity, from relatively mild food insecurity to prolonged clinical undernutrition (Nord et al., 2009; National Research Council, 2006).

The National Academies' Committee on National Statistics (CNSTAT) provided authoritative guidance on the definition and concept of hunger in official statistics in 2006. An independent panel of experts convened by CNSTAT concluded that in official statistics, resource-constrained hunger (i.e., physiological hunger resulting from food insecurity) "...should refer to a potential consequence of food insecurity that, because of prolonged, involuntary lack of food, results in discomfort, illness, weakness, or pain that goes beyond the usual uneasy sensation" (National Research Council, 2006, p. 48).

Validated methods have not yet been developed to measure the prevalence of resource-constrained hunger in this sense. Such measurement would require the collection of more detailed and extensive information on physiological experiences of individual household members than is available currently in nationally representative survey data.

Emerging Research on Children's Knowledge of and Experiences with Food Insecurity

USDA's measure of food insecurity among children relies on parental reports of food insecurity among children. Parents or caregivers are assumed to be knowledgeable about the food experiences of their children. Recent research has examined this assumption. Two studies investigated the food insecurity experiences of children, primarily adolescents, and compared children's reports of food insecurity with caregivers' reports of children's food insecurity. Both qualitative interview data (Fram et al., 2011) and quantitative survey data (Nord and Hanson, 2012) indicate that parents' reports of a child's food insecurity do not always correspond with the child's own reports.

Qualitative research on children ages 9-16 indicates that some youth take active roles in trying to reduce household food insecurity, sometimes without their parents' knowledge (Fram et al., 2011). Children reported strategies for reducing household food insecurity that included not asking for snacks, not eating between mealtimes, and trying to earn money for food. In some households, parents tried to hide household food insecurity and believed that they successfully shielded their children from food insecurity, but children were aware of the household's food insecurity and worried about a shortage of food; in some cases, children reported reducing their own food intake when they knew food was running low. That study did not administer the full household food security survey to adults and children, so it is unclear whether parents and children would have differed in their survey reports of food insecurity among children. The study did conclude that, at times, parents were unaware of the degree to which their children knew about household food insecurity and the degree to which children reduced their own food intake or took other steps to try to reduce household food insecurity. Earlier research also indicated that children were aware of adult attempts to hide food insecurity or to shield them from food insecurity (Connell et al., 2005).

Quantitative survey data from the National Health and Nutrition Examination Survey (NHANES) were used to examine agreement between adult caregiver reports of adolescent food insecurity and the adolescents' (ages 15-17) own reports of food insecurity (Nord and Hanson, 2012). Adolescent self-reported food insecurity was more common than parental reports of adolescent food insecurity. The study also examined dietary quality differences among adolescents and found that dietary quality was lowest for adolescents with both self-reported food insecurity and parental-reported adolescent food insecurity. Dietary quality was highest for adolescents with neither self-reported nor parental-reported food insecurity. Dietary quality was intermediate for adolescents whose self-reported and parental-reported food insecurity differed. There were no systematic differences in dietary quality when adolescents' and caregivers' reports of adolescent food insecurity disagreed, making it difficult to determine which report corresponded most accurately with the child's dietary intake.

A second study using NHANES data found that youth ages 12-17 were considerably less likely to be food insecure than adults in the same household, based on self-reported personal food insecurity of both youth and adults (Nord, 2013). The extent of the youth-adult gap in likelihood of self-reported food insecurity was greater when food insecurity was more severe. Depending on the method used to compare findings between that analysis and USDA's national food security statistics, the extent to which children are protected from food insecurity compared with adults in the same household was found to be somewhat greater or less than indicated by the national statistics, but any difference did not appear to be very large. However, even if national prevalence rates do not substantially misrepresent the extent of food insecurity among children, the extent of misreporting could substantially weaken associations of adult-reported food insecurity of children with children's health and developmental outcomes.

Associations between Children's Health/Development and Food Insecurity

A substantial and growing body of research has demonstrated associations between children's health, development, and well-being and measures of food security and food sufficiency. Food sufficiency—a condition closely related to food security—was assessed in several Federal surveys before the development of the food security measures and was used in much of the earlier research on outcomes of inadequate food access.[2] Most of the associations studied in earlier research focused on household-level food insecurity (or food insufficiency), not specifically on food insecurity among children. Most of these studies used cross-sectional data, which makes causality difficult to determine. More recent studies have advanced the research through expanded use of longitudinal data and measures of food insecurity among children. A wide range of methodologies and datasets have been used, and most studies controlled for confounding conditions, such as income, employment status, race, and ethnicity. These study findings are consistent with the hypothesis that food insecurity is a risk factor for the problematic outcomes studied. In most of these studies, the higher rates of problematic health and development outcomes for children were associated with food insecurity at the household level, regardless of whether there was evidence of food insecurity among children in the household.

Findings of studies on child health and development outcomes associated with food insecurity and food insufficiency are summarized in Appendix A. Although most of the studies found statistically significant associations between food insecurity and various outcomes for children, some of the associations were not statistically significant, and these findings are also shown in Appendix A. Statistically significant findings included associations of food insecurity or food insufficiency with:

- Poorer health of children and adolescents, as reported by parents;
- Lower bone mineral content in adolescent boys;
- Impaired development of non-cognitive abilities (i.e., interpersonal relations, self-control) among school-age children;
- Iron deficiency anemia among young children and adolescents;
- Insecure attachment and less advanced mental proficiency in toddlers;
- Higher rates of developmental risk among young children;
- More stomach aches, frequent headaches, and colds among children;
- Higher hospitalization rates among young children;
- Behavioral problems among 3-year-old children;
- Lower physical function among children ages 3-8;
- Poorer psychosocial function and psychosocial development among school-age children;
- Higher rates of depressive disorder and suicidal symptoms among adolescents;
- More anxiety and depression among school-age children;
- Higher numbers of chronic health conditions among children;
- More "internalizing" behavior problems (such as withdrawal or anxiety) among children;
- Lower math achievement and math progress in kindergartners;
- Lower math and reading gains from kindergarten to third grade; and
- Lower arithmetic scores and higher likelihood of repeating a grade among children ages 6-11.

Findings for food insecurity and children's weight status are less clear. Larson and Story (2011) conducted an extensive literature review of studies that analyzed this relationship and found that statistically significant findings were not in agreement. Additional research is needed to understand the reasons for these inconsistencies.

TRENDS IN FOOD INSECURITY IN HOUSEHOLDS WITH CHILDREN, 1999-2011

The prevalence of food insecurity in households with children increased from 1999 through the recession in 2001 (fig. 3). It continued to increase during 2002-04 despite renewed economic growth and then declined in 2005, remaining around that level through 2007. The prevalence of food insecurity in households with children increased substantially with the 2008 recession. In 2009, food insecurity in households with children reached a historic peak since Federal food security monitoring began in 1995, at just over 21 percent. It declined in 2010 and was essentially unchanged in 2011. From 1999 to 2011, the trends of food insecurity among children were similar to those for food insecurity of all household members.

The prevalence of very low food security among children varied little from 1999 to 2006, fluctuating between 0.5 and 0.7 percent. This rate increased to 0.8 percent in 2007, rose to a high of 1.3 percent in 2008, and declined to 1.0 percent in 2010 and 2011.

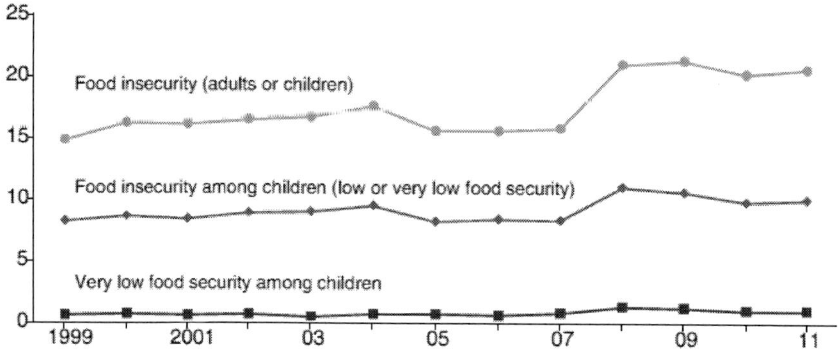

Source: USDA, Economic Research Service calculations based on Current Population Survey Food Security Supplement data.

Figure 3. Trends in food insecurity in households with children, 1999-2011.

USDA gives particular attention to food insecurity in households with children with annual household incomes less than 185 percent of the Federal poverty line, because these households may be eligible for food and nutrition assistance programs.[3] The income cutoff for participation in reduced-price school meals and WIC is 185 percent of the Federal poverty line. School-age children in households in this income range are likely to be eligible for free or reduced-price school meals. Households in this income range may be eligible for WIC benefits if they include children under the age of 5 or pregnant/postpartum women. Households with incomes less than 130 percent of the Federal poverty line may be eligible for SNAP benefits.

The prevalence of food insecurity for households with annual incomes less than 185 percent of the Federal poverty line was almost twice as high (40 percent in 2011) as that for all households with children. Trends over 1999-2011 in low-income households were generally similar to those in all households with children (fig. 4).

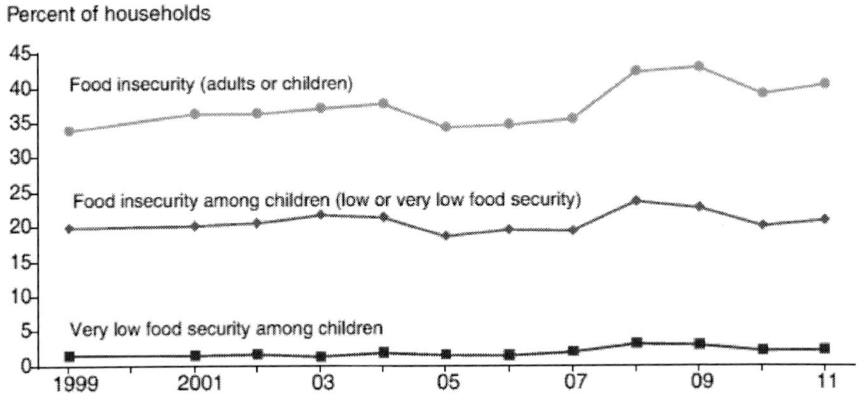

Source: USDA, Economic Research Service calculations based on Current Population Survey Food Security Supplement data.

Figure 4. Trends in food insecurity in households with children, with annual incomes less than 185 percent of the Federal poverty line, 1999-2011.

Food Insecurity Among Children in Selected Subpopulations, Average 2010-11

The economic and demographic circumstances of households determine their food security to a great extent. In this section, the prevalence and distribution of food insecurity among children is described across 10 sets of economic, demographic, and geographic characteristics that past research has found to be associated with food insecurity. Data for these analyses are from the December 2010 and December 2011 Current Population Survey Food Security Supplements. Data from 2 years were aggregated to provide more reliable estimates, especially for small subpopulations.

Three charts are presented for each set of household characteristics:

- **Bar chart:** depicts, for households with each characteristic (e.g., income level, disability status, etc.), the percentage of households with food-insecure children (households with food-insecure children include those with low and very low food security) and the percentage that had children with very low food security;
- **Pie chart 1:** shows the distribution of households with food insecurity among children across the characteristics; and
- **Pie chart 2:** shows the distribution of households with very low food security among children across the characteristics.

See Appendix B for the numbers underlying the graphic presentations in this section. The table in appendix B also includes statistics (not presented in the graphics) for the broader category of food insecurity that includes food insecurity among adults as well as children.

Household Income

Nearly 25 percent of households with annual incomes below the Federal poverty line had food insecurity among children in 2010-11 (fig. 5).[4] They made up 44 percent of all households with food insecurity among children and about 52 percent of households with very low food security among children.[5] The prevalence rate of food insecurity among children for households with annual incomes below the Federal poverty line was seven times that of households with annual incomes above 185 percent of the Federal poverty line.

Federal food and nutrition assistance programs may not be accessible to some households with food insecurity among children because their income exceeds the eligibility threshold.[6] Between 31 and 45 percent of households with food insecurity among children may not have been eligible for SNAP or for free school meals in 2010-11 because they had annual incomes higher than

130 percent of the poverty line—the income eligibility limit for these programs (the exact percentage of households ineligible for these programs cannot be determined because some households failed to report income). Some of these households may have been eligible for the programs because income eligibility is determined by monthly rather than annual income. Nevertheless, a large share of households with food insecurity among children likely was not eligible. Between 17 and 31 percent may not have been eligible for WIC or for reduced-price school lunches in 2010-11 because their incomes were above 185 percent of the poverty line, the income eligibility limit for these programs.

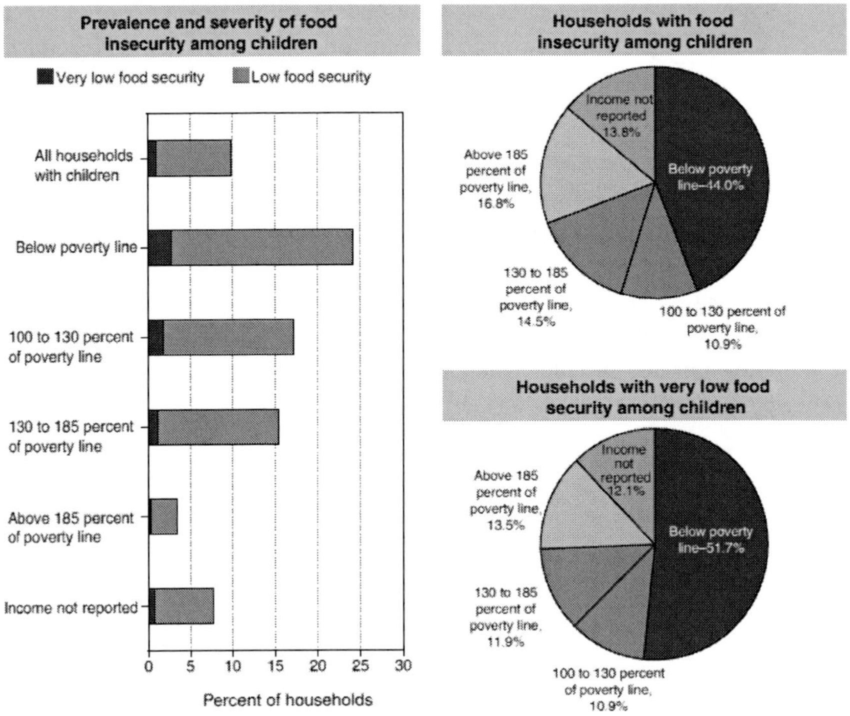

Source: USDA, Economic Research Service calculations based on Current Population Survey Food Security Supplement data.

Figure 5. Prevalence and distribution of food insecurity among children, by annual household income, 2010-11 average.

Employment and Labor Force Status of Adults in the Household

Rates of food insecurity among children were much higher for households with no employed adults (such as those with an unemployed adult and those with an adult who was unable to work due to disability) than for those with one or more adults employed full time (fig. 6).

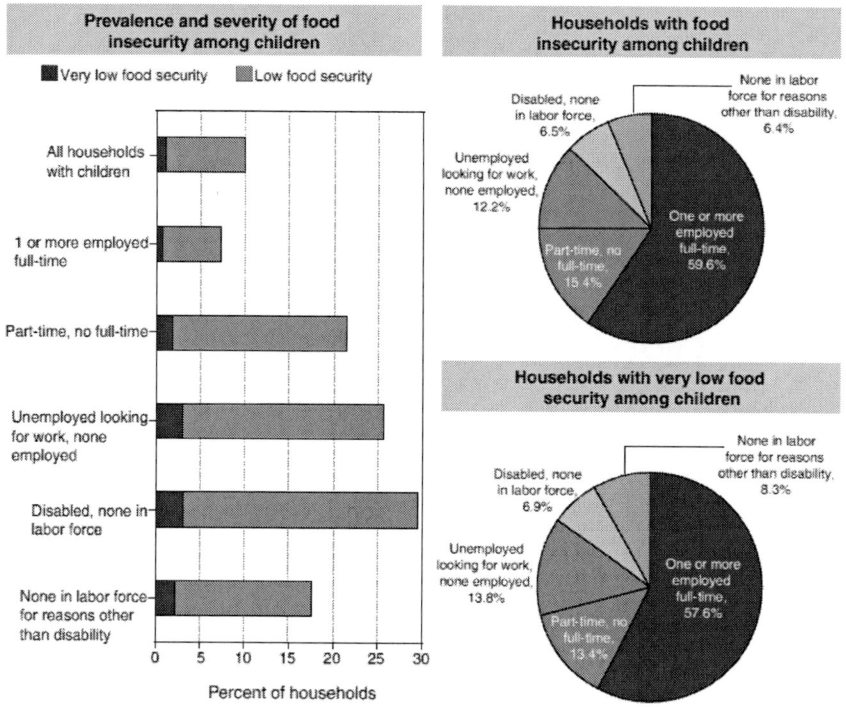

[1] Households classified as none in labor force for reasons other than disability had no adults that were identified as not in labor force due to disability. Disability identified in this figure is related to labor force status only. Adults with other reported disabilities are shown in figure 7.

Source: USDA, Economic Research Service calculations based on Current Population Survey Food Security Supplement data.

Figure 6. Prevalence and distribution of food insecurity among children, by employment and labor force status of adults in the household, 2010-11 average.[1]

Rates also were higher for households in which an adult was employed only part-time than in those with an adult employed full-time. About 60 percent of households with food insecurity among children had one or more full-time workers in 2010-11, and another 15 percent had one or more part-time workers. Together, the unemployed and not-in-labor-force-due-to-disability categories comprised about 19 percent of households with food insecurity among children and 21 percent of households with very low food security among children. (The next section has additional information on households with adults with disabilities.)

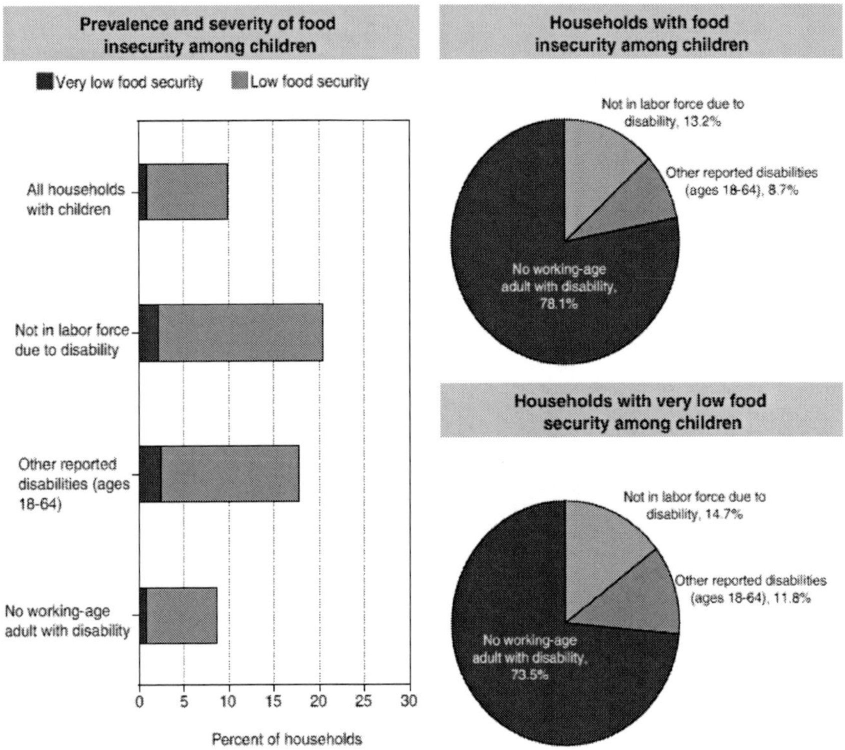

[1] Working-age adults with "other reported disabilities" were reported as having a vision, hearing, mental, physical, self-care, or going-outside-home disability but were not identified as being unable to work due to disability.

Source: USDA, Economic Research Service calculation based on Current Population Survey Food Security Supplement data.

Figure 7. Prevalence and distribution of food insecurity among children, by disability status of working-age adults in the household, 2010-11 average.[1]

Disability Status of Working-Age Adults in the Household

Food insecurity among children was more than twice as prevalent in households with an adult who was unable to work due to disability and in households with a working-age adult with other reported disabilities as in households with no working-age adult with a disability (fig. 7).[7] An estimated 22 percent of households with food insecurity among children had a working-age adult member (ages 18-64) with a disability. About 27 percent of households with very low food security among children included a working-age adult with a disability.

Educational Attainment of Adults in the Household

The prevalence of food insecurity among children is strongly associated with the education of adults in the household (fig. 8). Food insecurity was six and a half times as prevalent in households in which no adult had completed high school (24 percent) as in households where an adult had a 4-year college degree (almost 4 percent). In 49 percent of households with food insecurity among children and 46 percent of those with very low food security among children, no adult in the household had any education beyond high school.

Household Composition

Food insecurity among children was three times as prevalent in households headed by single women (19.2 percent) as in households headed by married couples (6.4 percent) (fig. 9). Children were food insecure in about 12 percent of households headed by unmarried cohabiting adults and in households headed by single men.[8] In spite of the lower rate of food insecurity among children in married-couple households, primarily due to their larger share of the population overall, married-couple households were a sizable minority (42 percent) of households with food insecurity among children, about equal to the proportion of households with food insecurity among children that were headed by a single woman (42 percent).

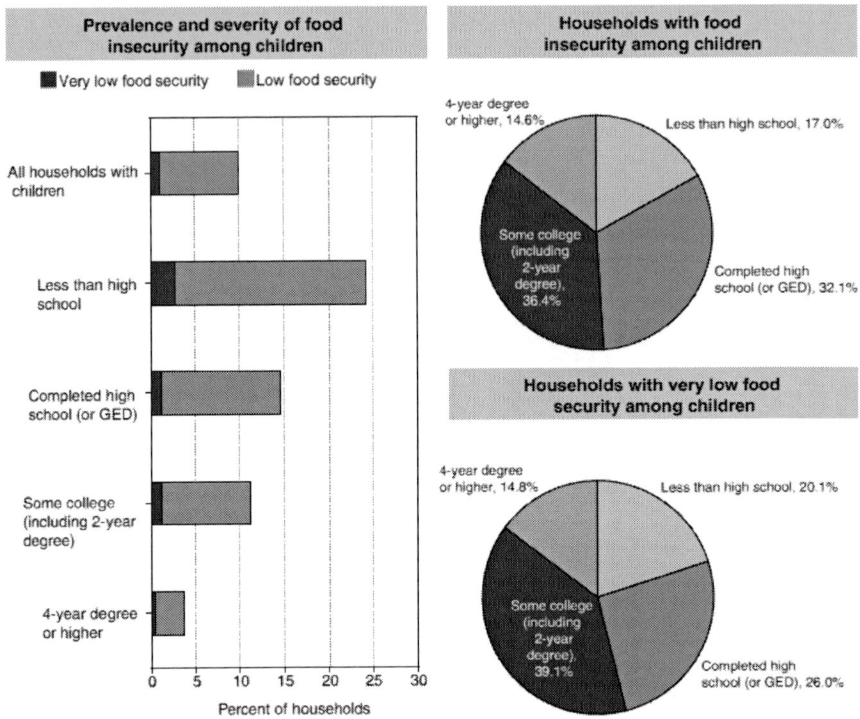

Source: USDA, Economic Research Service calculations based on Current Population Survey Food Security Supplement data.

Figure 8. Prevalence and distribution of food insecurity among children, by educational attainment of most educated adult in the household, 2010-11 average.

Race and Hispanic Ethnicity

Food insecurity among children was more than two and a half times as prevalent for households headed by non-Hispanic Black and Hispanic persons as for those headed by non-Hispanic Whites (fig. 10). Nevertheless, the highest percentage of households with food insecurity among children was headed by non-Hispanic Whites (about 39 percent) because of their larger share of the entire population. In the most severe category—households with very low food security among children— Hispanic households represented a larger share (about 36 percent) than any of the other race-ethnic groups in 2010-11.

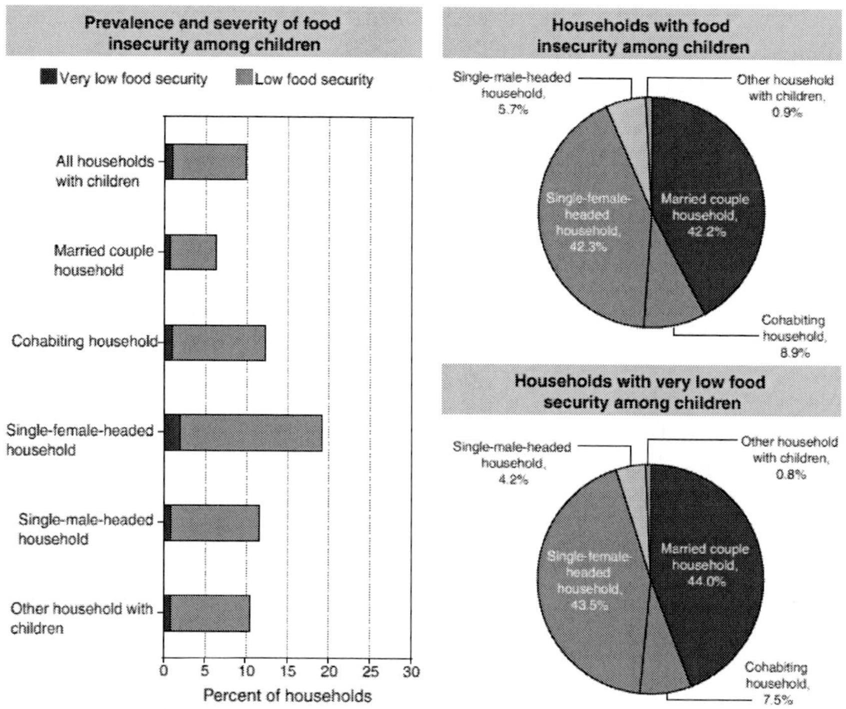

Source: USDA, Economic Research Service calculations based on Current Population Survey Food Security Supplement data.

Figure 9. Prevalence and distribution of food insecurity among children, by household composition, 2010-11 average.

Age of Oldest Child

Most parents attempt to shield their children from the more severe effects of food insecurity, even though they may have to reduce their own food intake to do so. Only about one out of six households with very low food security among adults had very low food security among children (analysis not shown).

Younger children are shielded from food insecurity to a greater extent than older children. The food security survey does not collect information on the food security of each individual child in the household, but examining the prevalence of food insecurity among children by the age of the oldest child in the household sheds light on the greater protection afforded to younger children (fig. 11). For example, food insecurity among children was almost twice as prevalent in households with teenage children as in households in which the oldest child was no older than age 4. Very low food security among children was more than three times as prevalent in households with teenage children as in households in which the oldest child was no older than age 4.[9]

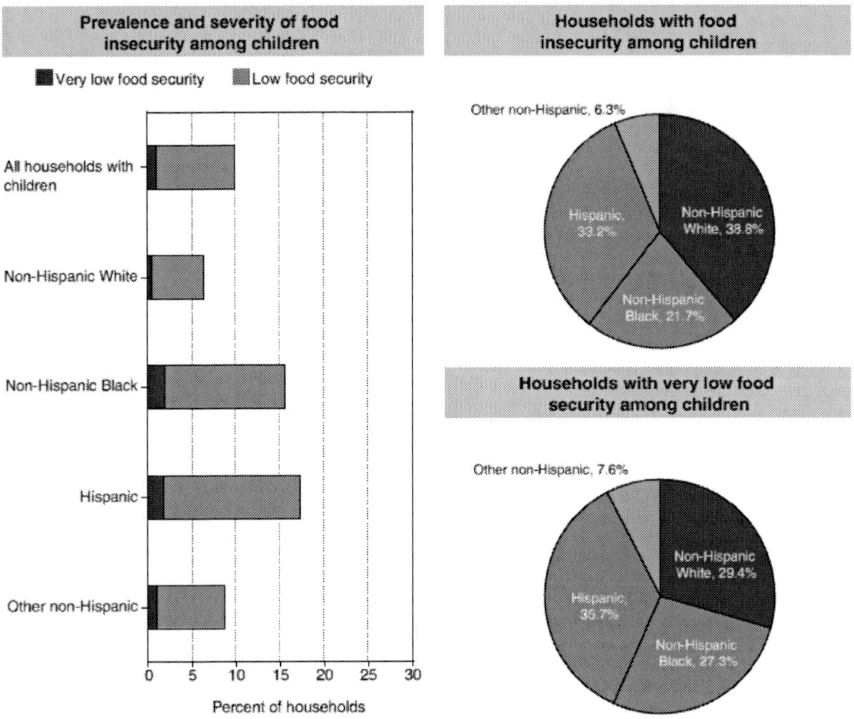

Source: USDA, Economic Research Service calculations based on Current Population Survey Food Security Supplement data.

Figure 10. Prevalence and distribution of food insecurity among children, by race and Hispanic ethnicity of household reference person, 2010-11 average.

Number of Children in the Household

Food insecurity among children was more prevalent in larger families, especially those with three or more children (fig. 12). The rates of food insecurity and very low food security among children were both twice as high in households with three or more children as in households with only one child. Households with food-insecure children were distributed about equally across households with one, two, and three or more children.

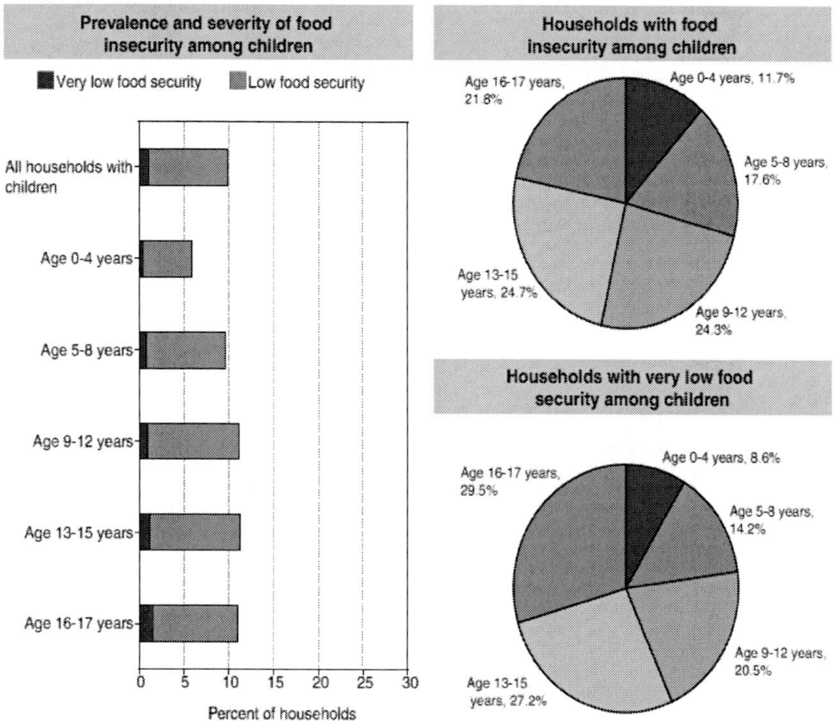

Source: USDA, Economic Research Service calculations based on Current Population Survey Food Security.

Figure 11. Prevalence and distribution of food insecurity among children, by age of oldest child in the household, 2010-11 average.

Residence Relative to Metropolitan Statistical Areas

Food insecurity among children was most prevalent in large cities of Metropolitan Statistical Areas (MSAs) followed by nonmetropolitan (largely rural) areas, and was least prevalent in the suburban and exurban commuting areas around large cities (fig. 13).[10] The largest shares of households with both food insecurity and low food security among children were in the principal cities of MSAs and the suburban and outlying commuting areas around MSAs.

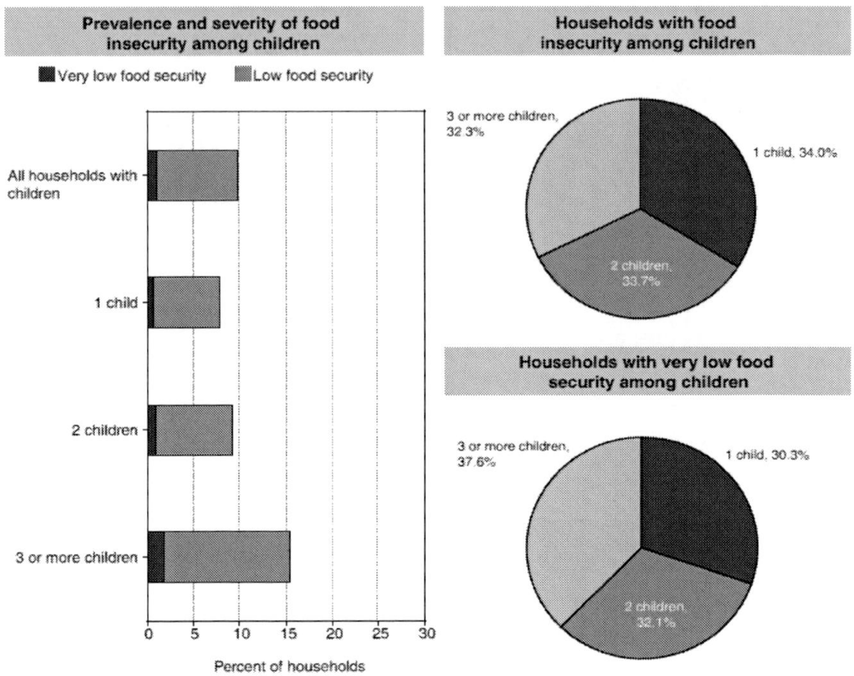

Source: USDA, Economic Research Service calculations based on Current Population Survey Food Security Supplement data.

Figure 12. Prevalence and distribution of food insecurity among children, by number of children in the household, 2010-11 average.

Residence by Census Region

The prevalence of food insecurity among children was higher in the West and South Census Regions than in the Midwest and Northeast (fig. 14). The prevalence of very low food security among children was highest in the South. Just over 40 percent of households with food insecure children and about 48 percent of households with very low food security among children were located in the South.

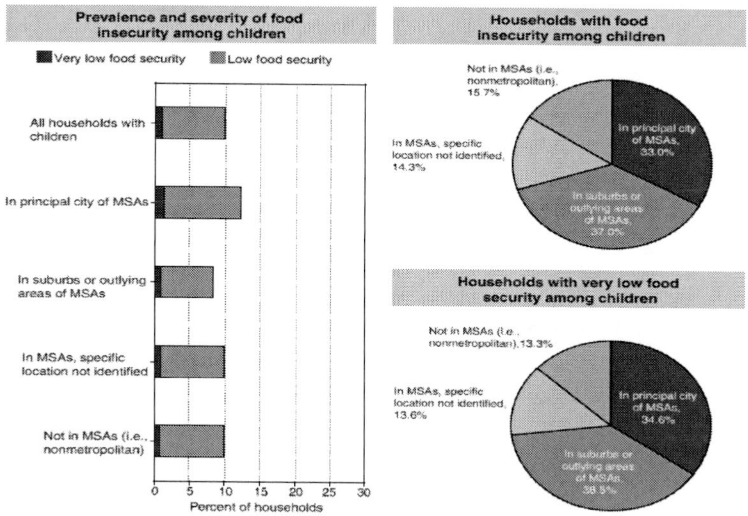

Source: USDA, Economic Research Service calculations based on Current Population Survey Food Security Supplement data.

Figure 13. Prevalence and distribution of food insecurity among children, by residence relative to Metropolitan Statistical Areas (MSAs), 2010-11 average.

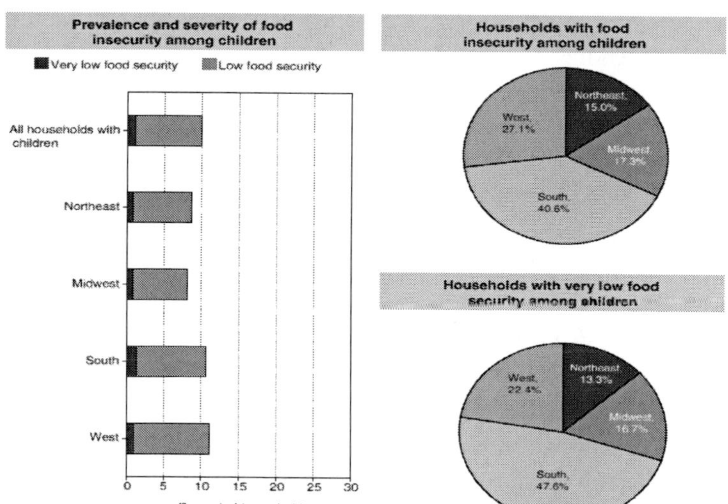

Source: USDA, Economic Research Service calculations based on Current Population Survey Food Security Supplement data.

Figure 14. Prevalence and distribution of food insecurity among children, by Census Region, 2010-11 average.

Food and Nutrition Assistance Program Participation and Children's Food Insecurity, Average 2010-11

Most food-insecure households with children received assistance from one or more of the three largest Federal food and nutrition assistance programs: the Supplemental Nutrition Assistance Program (SNAP, formerly called the Food Stamp Program), the National School Lunch Program, and the Special Supplemental Nutrition Assistance Program for Women, Infants, and Children (WIC). Table 1 and figure 15 show the prevalence of overall food insecurity and food insecurity among children for low-income households (households with children and annual incomes less than 185 percent of the Federal poverty line) participating in these programs.[11] The share of low-income food-insecure households with children and share of households with food insecurity among children participating in these programs are also shown.

These statistics come from a 30-day measure of food insecurity (covering mid-November to mid-December), rather than the standard 12-month measure, so that the period over which food security is assessed is more likely to match the period during which program benefits were received or not received. The prevalence of food insecurity is lower when assessed over a 30-day period, since some households were food insecure only in earlier months of the year. The prevalence of food insecurity in households with children and with annual incomes less than 185 percent of the Federal poverty line was 22.4 percent during the 30 days prior to the food security surveys in 2010 and 2011, compared with 39.6 percent that were food insecure at some time during the year (calculated from estimates shown in Appendix B). For food insecurity among children, the 30-day prevalence was 11.5 percent of low-income households compared with 20.4 percent when assessed over 12 months.

Households that did not receive assistance from any of these programs were generally more food secure than those that did. The prevalence of food insecurity was lower (about 12 percent) for nonparticipating households than for any recipient categories, likely reflecting the self-targeting of participation in these programs by the most food-needy households.

An estimated 84 percent of low-income households with food insecurity among children received assistance from one or more of the three largest Federal food assistance programs in 2010-11. About 70 percent of low-income households with food-insecure children received free or reduced-price school meals, including about 40 percent that received benefits from SNAP or WIC or both, in addition to school meals. Many households with food-insecure children in this income range (less than 185 percent of the Federal poverty line) were not eligible for all of these programs, and some were not eligible for any of them. Households with no children in school were not eligible for free or reduced-price school lunches. Among households with school-age children, 78.9 percent with food insecurity among children received free or reduced-price school meals (analysis not shown). Households with no children under age 5 were not eligible for WIC unless a woman in the household was pregnant. Among households with young children (ages 0-4), 58.2 percent with food insecurity among children participated in WIC (analysis not shown). About 28 percent of these low-income households reported annual incomes higher than 130 percent of the Federal poverty line (the gross income eligibility limit for SNAP); most of those were income-ineligible for SNAP.[12] Among households with incomes below 130 percent of the poverty line, nearly 50 percent with food insecurity among children participated in SNAP (table 2).

Table 1. Prevalence and distribution of food insecurity during the 30-day period ending in mid-December for low-income[1] households with children, by participation in selected Federal food assistance programs, 2010-11 average

	Households with food insecurity among adults or children		Households with food insecurity among children (low or very low food security among children)	
Characteristic	Prevalence[2]	Share[3]	Prevalence[4]	Share[5]
			Percent	
All low-income households with children[1]	22.4	100.0	11.5	100.0
Received SNAP in past 30 days	27.5	45.3	13.3	42.4
Received free or reduced price school lunch in past 30 days	27.8	66.2	15.3	70.3
Received WIC in past 30 days	26.3	25.3	13.4	25.0
Multiple-program patterns:[6]				
Received SNAP, free or reduced-price school lunch, and WIC	30.3	8.6	17.1	9.4
Received SNAP and free or reduced-price school lunch	29.1	24.6	14.7	24.0
Received SNAP and WIC	23.5	5.7	9.6	4.5
Received SNAP only	23.2	6.3	8.2	4.4
Received free or reduced-price school lunch and WIC	25.2	5.0	15.7	6.0
Received free or reduced-price school lunch only	26.5	27.8	15.2	30.6

Table 1. (Continued)

	Households with food insecurity among adults or children		Households with food insecurity among children (low or very low food security among children)	
Characteristic	Prevalence[2]	Share[3]	Prevalence[4]	Share[5]
			Percent	
Received WIC only	25.2	6.1	10.9	5.1
Received benefits from one or more of these programs	26.9	84.1	13.9	84.0
Did not receive benefits from any of these programs	12.3	15.9	6.4	16.0

SNAP = Supplemental Nutrition Assistance Program.

WIC = Special Supplemental Nutrition Program for Women, Infants, and Children.

[1]Analysis was limited to households with children and with annual incomes less than 185 percent of the Federal poverty line. Most households with incomes above that range were not asked whether they received benefits from food assistance programs. In 2011, the poverty line for a family of two adults and two children was an annual income of $22,811.

[2]Households with food insecurity among adults or children as a percentage of all households with the specified characteristic.

[3]Households with the specified characteristic and with food insecurity among adults or children as a percentage of all households with food insecurity among adults or children.

[4]Households with food insecurity among children as a percentage of all households with the specified characteristic.

[5]Households with the specified characteristic and with food insecurity among children as a percentage of all households with food insecurity among children.

[6]Percentages summed across multiple-program patterns may not exactly match those for SNAP, free or reduced-price school lunch, and WIC reported at the top of the table due to rounding. Also, some households only responded to questions about one or two programs but not all three, and their multiple-program participation could not be determined.

Source: USDA, Economic Research Service calculations based on Current Population Survey Food Security Supplement data.

Some households leave SNAP because their economic situation has improved enough to cover their food needs without assistance. For many SNAP recipients who exit the program, however, that does not seem to be the case. Households with children that received SNAP earlier in the year, but not in the 30 days prior to the food security survey, were more likely to be food insecure during that 30-day period (about 35 percent; table 2) than those still receiving benefits (approximately 28 percent), and much more likely to be food insecure than low-income households that did not receive SNAP benefits at any time during the year (nearly 20 percent). ERS research found that leaving SNAP was strongly associated with increases in income and full-time employment, suggesting that many food-insecure households that leave SNAP do so because they are no longer income-eligible (Nord and Coleman-Jensen, 2010). Even though these former participants appeared to be better off economically, they were still more likely to be food insecure after leaving SNAP.

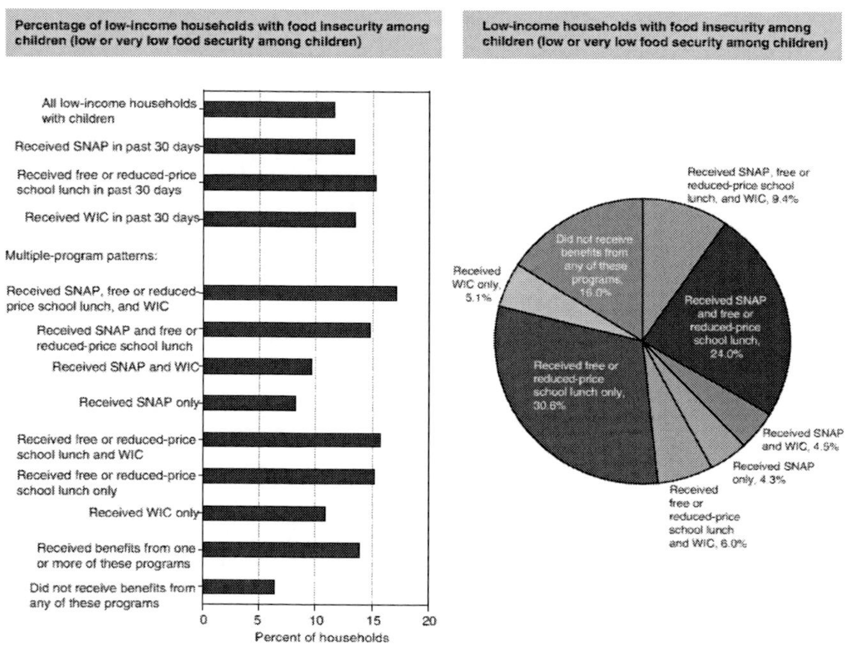

SNAP = Supplemental Nutrition Assistance Program.

WIC = Special Supplemental Nutrition Program for Women, Infants, and Children.

[1] Households with annual incomes less than 185 percent of the Federal poverty line. In 2011, the poverty line for a family of two adults and two children was an annual income of $22,811.

Source: USDA, Economic Research Service calculations based on Current Population Survey Food Security Supplement data.

Figure 15. Prevalence and distribution of food insecurity among children in low-income[1] households during the 30-day period prior to the food security survey, by participation in selected Federal food and nutrition assistance programs, 2010-11 average.

Table 2. Prevalence and distribution of food insecurity during the 30-day period ending in mid-December in households with children, with annual incomes less than 130 percent of the Federal poverty line,[1] by receipt of SNAP (food stamp) benefits, average 2010-11

	Households with food insecurity among adults or children		Households with food insecurity among children (low or very low food security among children)	
Characteristic	Prevalence[2]	Share[3]	Prevalence[4]	Share[5]
		Percent		
Received SNAP in past 30 days	27.7	52.2	13.7	49.9
Received SNAP in past 12 months, but not during the past 30 days	35.3	11.4	20.9	13.1
Did not receive SNAP at any time in past 12 months	19.6	36.3	10.4	37.1

SNAP = Supplemental Nutrition Assistance Program.

[1]In 2011, the Federal poverty line for a family of two adults and two children was an annual income of $22,811.

[2]Households with food insecurity among adults or children as a percentage of all households with the specified characteristic.

[3]Households with the specified characteristic and with food insecurity among adults or children as a percentage of all households with food insecurity among adults or children.

[4]Households with food insecurity among children as a percentage of all households with the specified characteristic.

[5]Households with the specified characteristic and with food insecurity among children as a percentage of all households with food insecurity among children.

Source: USDA, Economic Research Service calculations based on Current Population Survey Food Security Supplement data.

Food Insecurity in Households with Children, by State, 2003-11 Average

Data from nine national surveys (December of each year in 2003-11) were combined to provide sufficient sample sizes (numbers of households interviewed) for reliable State-level estimates (table 3 and fig. 16). The long time period for these State-level statistics should be kept in mind when interpreting the statistics, as conditions in some States may have changed during that time. Even with data from nine surveys, the prevalence of very low food security among children could not be estimated reliably for some States and is not reported in table 3.[13]

The prevalence of food insecurity in households with children ranged from almost 11 percent in New Hampshire to about 24 percent in Texas. Taking into account margins of error due to sampling variation, the prevalence of food insecurity in households with children was below the national average (18.3 percent) in 19 States, above the national average in 14 States and the District of Columbia, and near the national average (i.e., the difference from the national average was not statistically significant) in 17 States. The percentage of households with food insecurity among children ranged from about 5 percent in New Hampshire to almost 13 percent in Texas.

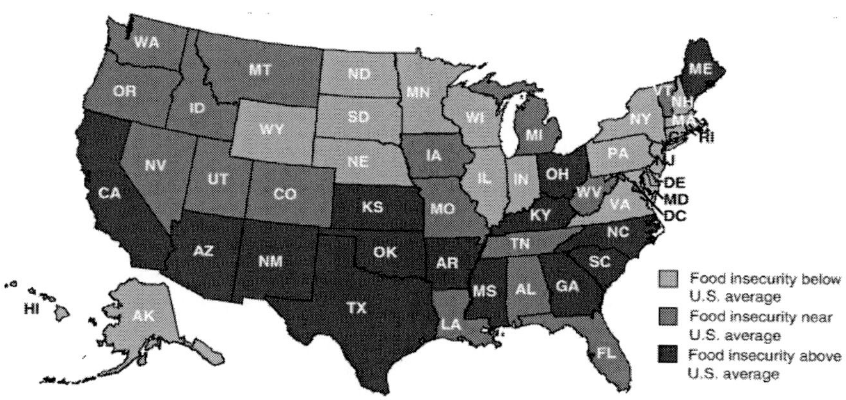

Source: USDA, Economic Research Service calculations based on Current Population Survey Food Security Supplement data.

Figure 16. Prevalence of food insecurity (adults or children) in households with children, 2003-11 average.

Table 3. Prevalence of food insecurity in households with children, by State, average 2003-11[1]

	Number of households with children		Households with food insecurity among adults or children (low or very low food security)		Households with food insecurity among children (low or very low food security among children)	
State	Average 2003-11	Interviewed	Prevalence	Margin of error[2]	Prevalence	Margin of error[2]
	Number	*Number*	*Percent*	*Percentage points*	*Percent*	*Percentage points*
U.S. total	**39,573,000**	**133,083**	**18.3**	**0.22**	**9.4**	**0.17**
AK	94,000	1,962	16.0*	1.77	8.0*	1.13

Table 3. (Continued)

	Number of households with children		Households with food insecurity among adults or children (low or very low food security)		Households with food insecurity among children (low or very low food security among children)	
State	Average 2003-11	Interviewed	Prevalence	Margin of error[2]	Prevalence	Margin of error[2]
	Number	*Number*	*Percent*	*Percentage points*	*Percent*	*Percentage points*
AL	593,000	1,526	20.1	1.90	9.3	1.76
AR	378,000	1,574	21.8*	2.77	11.5*	1.88
AZ	817,000	1,741	21.5*	1.87	10.9*	1.19
CA	4,901,000	11,056	19.2*	0.78	10.8*	0.42
CO	662,000	2,959	17.0	1.58	8.8	0.94
CT	465,000	2,747	14.7*	1.29	8.0*	0.98
DC	60,000	1,197	21.7*	2.24	11.2*	1.64
DE	116,000	1,925	12.7*	1.13	7.0*	0.79
FL	2,173,000	4,692	18.4	0.87	9.4	0.66
GA	1,311,000	2,901	20.5*	1.44	10.5*	0.95
HI	155,000	1,903	15.2*	1.41	8.4*	0.93
IA	377,000	2,464	17.3	1.29	8.3*	0.86
ID	208,000	1,760	18.7	1.06	8.7	1.40
IL	1,698,000	4,285	15.3*	1.01	7.4*	0.73
IN	847,000	2,231	16.1*	1.54	7.8*	1.27
KS	378,000	2,173	19.8*	1.53	9.3	1.21
KY	559,000	1,957	19.9*	1.62	10.0	1.12
LA	609,000	1,351	17.1	1.47	9.0	1.16
MA	848,000	2,093	12.7*	1.40	7.1*	1.05
MD	741,000	2,900	14.4*	1.29	7.9*	0.86
ME	158,000	2,329	19.8*	1.47	10.3	1.12
MI	1,293,000	3,238	17.1	1.79	8.0*	0.99
MN	659,000	3,108	13.6*	1.24	7.1*	1.09
MO	777,000	2,300	18.6	1.66	9.0	1.41
MS	395,000	1,280	22.1*	2.22	12.4*	2.18
MT	115,000	1,266	19.2	2.29	9.0	1.36
NC	1,160,000	2,682	20.7*	1.77	10.2	1.02
ND	83,000	1,825	11.1*	1.37	5.8*	0.80
NE	237,000	2,098	16.1*	1.22	8.1*	0.76
NH	166,000	2,700	10.7*	0.90	5.1*	0.67
NJ	1,172,000	2,896	14.4*	1.67	7.4*	1.06
NM	261,000	1,270	21.9*	1.87	12.4*	1.72
NV	327,000	2,164	17.7	2.11	9.5	1.48
NY	2,452,000	5,291	17.2*	0.83	9.5	0.60
OH	1,522,000	3,854	19.8*	1.45	8.6	0.85
OK	487,000	1,762	21.0*	1.79	11.4*	1.25
OR	462,000	1,852	19.2	1.94	10.4	1.39
PA	1,555,000	3,949	16.9*	1.04	7.9*	0.72

	Number of households with children		Households with food insecurity among adults or children (low or very low food security)		Households with food insecurity among children (low or very low food security among children)	
State	Average 2003-11	Interviewed	Prevalence	Margin of error[2]	Prevalence	Margin of error[2]
	Number	*Number*	*Percent*	*Percentage points*	*Percent*	*Percentage points*
RI	144,000	2,255	18.4	1.76	9.8	1.56
SC	563,000	1,784	20.4*	1.33	9.8	1.14
SD	100,000	2,045	15.5*	1.69	7.9*	1.15
TN	796,000	1,785	19.4	1.83	10.1	1.04
TX	3,371,000	7,217	23.5*	0.78	12.8*	0.58
UT	384,000	1,978	17.4	1.72	9.0	1.35
VA	1,004,000	2,700	12.4*	1.00	6.2*	0.71
VT	79,000	1,771	17.4	2.02	8.0	1.58
WA	841,000	2,409	18.3	1.67	8.7	1.17
WI	724,000	2,569	15.4*	1.10	7.7*	0.82
WV	226,000	1,488	17.0	2.18	7.4*	1.28
WY	70,000	1,821	15.8*	1.57	7.9*	0.88

*Difference from U.S. average was statistically significant with 90-percent confidence ($t > 1.645$).

[1] Totals exclude households whose food security status is unknown because they did not give a valid response to any of the questions in the food security scale. Each year, these represented about 0.3 percent of all households.

[2] Margin of error with 90-percent confidence (1.645 times the standard error of the estimated prevalence rate).

Source: USDA, Economic Research Service calculations based on Current Population Survey Food Security Supplement data.

CONCLUSION

In the wake of the economic downturn that began in late 2007, food insecurity in households with children remains near the highest level observed since monitoring began in 1995. In 2011, 20.6 percent of households with children were food insecure at some time during the year. In about half of those households, only adults were food insecure; in the other half, children were also food insecure. In 1.0 percent of households with children, one or more of the children experienced very low food security.

Results from this study suggest that employment is a key determinant of food insecurity in households with children. Full-time job opportunities, work supports (e.g., tax credits and child care assistance), and employee benefits (e.g., health insurance) may reduce food insecurity. In 2010-11, food insecurity among children was three and a half times as prevalent for households headed by an unemployed adult as for households headed by one or more full-time employed adults. However, 75 percent of households with food-insecure children had one or more adults in the labor force, with about 60 percent having at least one full-time worker and an additional 15 percent having one or more part-time workers. In 2006-07, before the economic downturn, a higher percentage of households with food-insecure children had at least one full-time worker (67 percent), and a lower percentage had one or more part-time workers (10 percent; Nord, 2009).

Educational attainment is also strongly associated with food insecurity in households with children. Food insecurity among children was six and a half times as prevalent for households headed by an adult with less than a high school diploma as for households headed by an adult with at least a 4-year college degree. Adult education and job training programs may help adults with low levels of education to improve their employment status and household food security.

Disabilities are an important risk factor for food insecurity. Access to disability assistance programs, work supports, healthcare, and other assistance for adults with disabilities may reduce the incidence and severity of food insecurity for a substantial share of those that are currently food insecure (Coleman-Jensen and Nord, 2013). Current benefit levels in disability assistance programs (such as Supplemental Security Income or SSI) appear inadequate to ensure food security for those affected by disabilities. Food insecurity was twice as prevalent for households with children that included adults who were unable to work due to disabilities and for those with working-age adults with other reported disabilities, even if they were not reported to be unable to work because of disabilities, as for households with children in which no working-age adults reported a disability.

In 2010-11, Federal food and nutrition assistance programs provided benefits to 84.1 percent of low-income (less than 185 percent of the poverty line) food-insecure households with children. Many households received assistance from multiple programs, although about 28 percent reported receiving only free or reduced-price school meals. The free or reduced-price school meals program reaches a larger share of food-insecure households with children than either the SNAP or WIC programs. It is worth noting that participation in food and nutrition assistance programs, especially SNAP, increased with the onset of the economic downturn. In 2006-07, about 39 percent of food-insecure households with children received SNAP (Nord,

2009). In 2010-11, about 45 percent of food-insecure households with children received SNAP.

Low-income households that did not receive assistance from any of the food and nutrition assistance programs were less likely to be food insecure (just over 12 percent) than those that did receive assistance (23-30 percent, depending on the mix of programs). The lower prevalence of food insecurity among income-eligible nonparticipants suggests that many of these households were able to meet their food needs without assistance. About one in five food-insecure households with children had annual incomes above 185 percent of the poverty line. Many of these households may not have been eligible to receive free or reduced-price school lunches or assistance from the WIC program, and most were probably not eligible to receive SNAP benefits.[14]

As food insecurity prevalence rates hover around historic highs since food security monitoring began, and new research finds that children living in food-insecure households face elevated risks of negative health and development outcomes compared with children in otherwise similar food-secure households, the impetus to understand and address the underlying causes of food insecurity in households with children has increased. For example, in the 2010 Healthy, Hunger-Free Kids Act, Congress allocated $10 million for research into the causes and consequences of childhood hunger and food insecurity, with the research beginning in FY 2013. This report lays the foundation for such research by identifying the populations most at risk of childhood food insecurity.

References

Alaimo, Katherine, Christine M. Olson, and Edward A. Frongillo Jr. 2001a. "Food insufficiency and American school-aged children's cognitive, academic, and psychosocial development," *Pediatrics* 108(1): 44-53.

Alaimo, Katherine, Christine M. Olson, and Edward A. Frongillo Jr. 2001b. "Low family income and food insufficiency in relation to overweight in US children," *Archives of Pediatrics and Adolescent Medicine* 155(10): 1161-67.

Alaimo, Katherine, Christine M. Olson, and Edward A. Frongillo Jr. 2002. "Family food insufficiency, but not low family income, is positively associated with dysthymia and suicide symptoms in adolescents," *The Journal of Nutrition* 132(4): 719-25.

Alaimo, Katherine, Christine M. Olson, Edward A. Frongillo Jr., and Ronette R. Briefel. 2001. "Food insufficiency, family income, and health in US preschool and school-aged children," *American Journal of Public Health* 91(5): 781-86.

Bhargava, Alok, Dean Jolliffe, and Larry L. Howard. 2008. "Socio-economic, behavioural and environmental factors predicted body weights and household food insecurity scores in the Early Childhood Longitudinal Study-Kindergarten," *British Journal of Nutrition* 100(2): 438-44.

Bronte-Tinkew, Jacinta, Martha Zaslow, Randolph Capps, Allison Horowitz, and Michelle McNamara. 2007. "Food insecurity works through depression, parenting, and infant feeding to influence overweight and health in toddlers," *The Journal of Nutrition* 137(9): 2160-65.

Casey, Patrick H., Kitty L. Szeto, James M. Robbins, Janice E. Stuff, Carol Connell, Jeffrey Gossett, and Pippa M. Simpson. 2005. "Child health-related quality of life and household food security," *Archives of Pediatric and Adolescent Medicine* 159(1): 51-6.

Chilton, Mariana, Maureen M. Black, Carol Berkowitz, Patrick H. Casey, John Cook, Ruth Rose Jacobs, Alan Meyers, Deborah A. Frank, Diana Cutts, Timothy Heeren, Stephanie Ettinger de Cuba, and Sharon Coleman. 2009. "Food insecurity and risk of poor health among US-born children of immigrants," *American Journal of Public Health* 99(3): 556-62.

Coleman-Jensen, Alisha, and Mark Nord. 2013. *Food Insecurity Among Households With Working-Age Adults With Disabilities*, ERR-144, U.S. Department of Agriculture, Economic Research Service, http://www.ers.usda.gov/publications/err-economic-research-report/err 144.aspx.

Coleman-Jensen, Alisha, Mark Nord, Margaret Andrews, and Steven Carlson. 2012. *Household Food Security in the United States in 2011*, ERR-141, U.S. Department of Agriculture, Economic Research Service, http://ers.usda.gov/publications/err-economic-research-report/err141.aspx.

Connell, Carol L., Kristi L. Lofton, Kathy Yadrick, and Timothy A. Rehner. 2005. "Children's experiences of food insecurity can assist in understanding its effect on their well-being," *The Journal of Nutrition* 135(7): 1683-90.

Cook, John T., Deborah A. Frank, Carol Berkowitz, Maureen M. Black, Patrick H. Casey, Diana B. Cutts, Alan F. Meyers, Nieves Zaldivar, Anne Skalicky, Suzette Levenson, Tim Heeren, and Mark Nord. 2004. "Food insecurity is associated with adverse health outcomes among human infants and toddlers," *The Journal of Nutrition* 134: 1432-38.

DeNavas-Walt, Carmen, Bernadette D. Proctor, and Jessica C. Smith. 2012. "Income, poverty, and Health Insurance Coverage in the United States: 2011," *Current Population Reports*, P60-243, U.S. Department of Commerce, U.S. Census Bureau, http://www.census.gov/prod/2012pubs/p60-243.pdf.

Eicher-Miller, Heather A., April C. Mason, Connie M. Weaver, George P. McCabe, and Carol J. Boushey. 2009. "Food insecurity is associated with iron deficiency anemia in US adolescents," *The American Journal of Clinical Nutrition* 90(5): 1358-71.

Eicher-Miller, Heather A., April C. Mason, Connie M. Weaver, George P. McCabe, and Carol J. Boushey. 2011. "Food insecurity is associated with diet and bone mass disparities in early adolescent males but not females in the United States," *The Journal of Nutrition* 141(9): 1738-45.

Fram, Maryah Stella, Edward A. Frongillo, Sonya J. Jones, Roger C. Williams, Michael P. Burke, Kendra P. DeLoach, and Christine E. Blake. 2011. "Children are aware of food insecurity and take responsibility for managing food resources," *The Journal of Nutrition* 141(6): 1114-19.

Hernandez, Daphne C., and Alison Jacknowitz. 2009. "Transient, but not persistent, adult food insecurity influences toddler development," *The Journal of Nutrition* 139(8): 1517-24.

Howard, Larry L. 2011a. "Does food insecurity at home affect non-cognitive performance at school? A longitudinal analysis of elementary student classroom behavior," *Economics of Education Review* 30(1): 157-76.

Howard, Larry L. 2011b. "Transitions between food insecurity and food security predict children's social skill development during elementary school," *The British Journal of Nutrition* 105(12): 1852-60.

Jyoti, Diana F., Edward A. Frongillo, and Sonya J. Jones. 2005. "Food insecurity affects school children's academic performance, weight gain, and social skills," *The Journal of Nutrition* 135: 2831-39.

Kirkpatrick, Sharon I., Lynn McIntyre , and Melissa L. Potestio. 2010. "Child hunger and long-term adverse consequences for health," *Archives of Pediatrics and Adolescent Medicine* 164(8): 754-62.

Kleinman, Ronald E., J. Michael Murphy, Michelle Little, Maria Pagano, Cheryl A. Wehler, Kenneth Regal, and Michael S. Jellinek. 1998. "Hunger in Children in the United States: Potential Behavioral and Emotional Correlates," *Pediatrics* 101(1):e3.

Larson, Nicole I., and Mary T. Story. 2011. "Food insecurity and weight status among U.S. children and families. A review of the literature," *American Journal of Preventive Medicine* 40(2): 166-73.

National Research Council. 2006. *Food Insecurity and Hunger in the United States: An Assessment of the Measure*, Committee on National Statistics, Panel to Review the U.S. Department of Agriculture's Measurement of Food Insecurity and Hunger, Gooloo S. Wunderlich and Janet L. Norwood (Eds.), Washington, DC: The National Academies Press.

Nord, Mark. 2013 (Forthcoming). "Youth are less likely to be food insecure than adults in the same household," *Journal of Hunger and Environmental Nutrition*.

Nord, Mark. 2009. *Food Insecurity in Households with Children: Prevalence, Severity, and Household Characteristics*, EIB-56, U.S. Department of Agriculture, Economic Research Service, http://ers.usda.gov/publications /eibeconomic-information-bulletin/eib56.aspx.

Nord, Mark, and Alisha Coleman-Jensen. 2010. "Food insecurity after leaving SNAP," *Journal of Hunger & Environmental Nutrition* 5(4): 434-53.

Nord, Mark, and Karla Hanson. 2012. "Adult caregiver reports of adolescents' food security do not agree well with adolescents' own reports," *Journal of Hunger & Environmental Nutrition* 7(4): 363-80.

Nord, Mark, Max Finberg, and James McLaughlin. 2009. "What should the government mean by hunger?" *Journal of Hunger & Environmental Nutrition* 4(1):1-28.

Oliveira, Victor. 2013. *The Food Assistance Landscape: FY 2012 Annual Report*, EIB-109, U.S. Department of Agriculture, Economic Research Service, http:// www.ers.usda.gov/publications/eib-economic-information-bulletin/eib109.aspx.

Park, Kyong, Margaret Kersey, Joni Geppert, Mary Story, Diana Cutts, and John H. Himes. 2009. "Household food insecurity is a risk factor for iron-deficiency anemia in a multi-ethnic, low-income sample of infants and toddlers," *Public Health Nutrition* 12(11): 2120-28.

Rose-Jacobs, Ruth, Maureen M. Black, Patrick H. Casey, John T. Cook, Diana B. Cutts, Mariana Chilton, Timothy Heeren, Suzette M. Levenson, Alan F. Meyers, and Deborah A. Frank. 2008. "Household Food Insecurity: Associations with At-Risk Infant and Toddler Development," *Pediatrics* 121(1): 65-72.

Ryu, Jeong-Hee, and Judith S. Bartfeld. 2012. "Household food insecurity during childhood and subsequent health status: The Early Childhood Longitudinal Study - Kindergarten Cohort," *American Journal of Public Health* 102(11): e50-5.

Skalicky, Anne, Alan F. Meyers, William G. Adams, Zhaoyan Yang, John T. Cook, and Deborah A. Frank. 2006. "Child food insecurity and iron

deficiency anemia in low-income infants and toddlers in the United States," *Maternal and Child Health Journal* 10(2): 177-85.
Slack, Kristen S. and Joan Yoo. 2005. "Food hardship and child behavior problems among low-income children," *Social Service Review* 79(3): 511-36.
Weinreb, Linda, Cheryl Wehler, Jennifer Perloff, Richard Scott, David Hosmer, Linda Sagor, and Craig Gundersen. 2002. "Hunger: Its impact on children's health and mental health," *Pediatrics* 110(4): e41.
Whitaker, Robert C., Shannon M. Phillips, and Sean M. Orzol. 2006. "Food insecurity and the risks of depression and anxiety in mothers and behavior problems in their preschool-aged children," *Pediatrics* 118(3): e859-68.
Winicki, Joshua, and Kyle Jemison. 2003. "Food insecurity and hunger in the kindergarten classroom: Its effect on learning and growth," *Contemporary Economic Policy* 21(2): 145-57.
Zaslow, Martha, Jacinta Bronte-Tinkew, Randolph Capps, Allison Horowitz, Kristin A. Moore, and Debra Weinstein. 2009. "Food security during infancy: Implications for attachment and mental proficiency in toddlerhood," *Maternal and Child Health Journal* 13(1): 66-80.

APPENDIX A: PREVIOUS STUDY FINDINGS

Findings from selected studies on the effects of food insecurity and food insufficiency on children's health, development, and well-being (statistically significant associations, with controls included in the model, are shaded)

Introductory notes:

- Most of the associations reported here are based on food insecurity or food insufficiency at the household level, not on food insecurity among children. Many presumed effects of household food insecurity on children appear even though the children themselves may not experience reductions in diet quality or quantity.
- Studies controlled for income and other household characteristics likely to confound the relationships of interest.
- The studies are listed by year of publication and alphabetically by author.

Appendix Table A.

Condition studied	Population	Finding	Data[1]	Comments	Citation
Parent reported gen eral health status of child on a 5-point scale ranging from poor to excellent	Children in kindergarten through eighth grade	Persistent food insecurity (3 or 4 observa tion years) was associated with lower health status in eighth grade.	ECLS-K	The study controlled for child's kindergar-ten health status and parental depression.	Ryu and Bartfeld, 2012
		Transient food insecurity (1 or 2 observa tion years) was not associated with health status at eighth grade.			
Bone mineral content	Boys ages 8-11	Significantly lower bone mineral content in total body, trunk, lumbar spine, pelvis, and left arm in households with food insecurity among children.	NHANES		Eicher-Miller et al., 2011
	Boys ages 12-19 and girls ages 8-19	No statistically significant association.			
USDA Food Guide recommended servings of dairy and estimated average requirement for calcium intake.	Boys ages 8-11	2.5 times more likely to report less than the recommended servings of dairy and 2.3 times more likely to have calcium intake below the estimated average requirement.			
	Boys ages 12-19 and girls ages 8-19	No statistically significant association.			
Noncognitive abilities (teacher-reported: interpersonal relations, self-control, approach es to learning, and externalizing problem behavior)	Children in first, third, and fifth grade	Transition from food-insecure household in first grade to food-secure household in third grade was negatively associated with interpersonal relations, self-control, and approaches to learning persisting through fifth grade.	ECLS-K	Controls for county characteristics in addition to household characteristics.	Howard, 2011a
		Contemporaneous household food insecurity was negatively associated with interpersonal relations, self-control, and approaches to learning.			

Condition studied	Population	Finding	Data[1]	Comments	Citation
		No statistically significant association between food insecurity and externalizing problem behavior.			
Social skills (teacher reported: interpersonal relationships, self- control, approaches to learning, externalizing problem behavior)	Girls in first, third, and fifth grade	Contemporaneous household food insecurity was negatively associated with composite social skills scores, self-control and approaches to learning scores.	ECLS-K	Controls for county characteristics in addition to household characteristics.	Howard, 2011b
		Transitions between food insecurity and food security were not statistically significantly associated with social skills scores.			
	Boys in first, third, and fifth grade	Transitioning from food insecurity in first grade to food security in third grade was negatively associated with composite social skills scores, self-control, and approaches to learning scores.			
		Other transitions between food insecurity and food security were not statistically significantly associated with social skills scores. There was no statistically significant association between food insecurity and social skills measured contempora- neously.			
General health (parent reported)	Children ages 10-15	Poor or fair (vs. excellent, very good, or good) health 2.48 times more likely for children classified as hungry. Poor or fair health 4.73 times as likely for children who have experienced two or more episodes of hunger than those that have never experienced hunger.	NLSCY[2]	Controlled for baseline health status and chronic health conditions. In analyses stratified by gender rather than age, associations were stronger for girls than for boys.	Kirkpatrick et al., 2010
	Children ages 16-21	No statistically significant association.			

Appendix Table A. (Continued)

Condition studied	Population	Finding	Data[1]	Comments	Citation
Chronic health conditions (heart condition, cerebral palsy, epi lepsy, kidney disease, asthma, bronchitis, or allergies)	Children ages 10-15	No statistically significant association.			
	Children ages 16-21	Higher odds of having any chronic health condition or of having asthma (considered separately from other health conditions) among youth with two or more episodes of hunger.			
General health (parent reported)	Children ages 0-36 months	Poor or fair (versus excellent, very good, or good) health 1.74 times more likely in food-insecure households	Children's Health-Watch (formerly C-SNAP)		Chilton et al., 2009
		Food insecurity mediated the association between immigrant status of mothers and fair or poor health among children.			
Iron deficiency anemia	Children ages 3-5	10.71 times as likely for children in households with food insecurity among children	NHANES	Wide confidence inter-vals for the estimates for children ages 3-5 and 6-11; although statistically significant, the estimate should be interpreted with caution.	Eicher-Miller et al., 2009
	Children ages 6-11	8.05 times as likely for children in households with food insecurity among children			
	Children ages 12-15	2.95 times as likely for adolescents in households with food insecurity among children.			
	Children ages 16-19	No statistically significant association.			

Condition studied	Population	Finding	Data[1]	Comments	Citation
Iron deficiency	Children ages 6-11	49 percent less likely among children in households with food insecurity among children.		Unexpected finding that children from households with food security among children were more likely to be iron deficient than children from households with food insecurity among children.	
	Children ages 3-5 and ages 12-19	No statistically significant association.			
Estimated average requirement (EAR) for iron intake	Children ages 16-19	Dietary iron intake 1.87 times below the EAR among youth from food-insecure households.			
	Children ages 3-15	No statistically significant association.			
Condition studied	Population	Finding	Data[1]	Comments	Citation
Cognitive scores	Children age 9 months and 24 months	Children in households with food insecu- rity among adults at wave 2 (when child was 24 months old) scored 1.5 points lower on cognitive scores at 24 months. In separate analyses of boys and girls, the effect on boys' scores was not statisti cally significant, but girls in food-insecure households scored 2.33 points lower.	ECLS-B	Data were collected at two time points, or waves. Wave 1 of data collection	Hernandez and Jacknowitz, 2009

Appendix Table A. (Continued)

Condition studied	Population	Finding	Data[1]	Comments	Citation
				was conducted when the child was 9 months old. Wave 2 of data collection was conducted when the child was 24 months old. Food insecurity was assessed at both waves, while the outcomes of interest were assessed at wave 2.	
		Food insecurity among adults at wave 1 (when child was 9 months old) was not significantly associated with child cogni tive scores at wave 2 (age 24 months). Food insecurity at both waves was not associated with scores at wave 2.		Counterintuitive finding that food insecurity among adults at wave 2 affected child's cog-nitive scores, but food insecurity at both wave 1 and at wave 2 did not significantly affect cognitive scores.	

Condition studied	Population	Finding	Data[1]	Comments	Citation
Motor scores		No statistically significant association between child motor scores at wave 2 and food insecurity among adults measured at wave 1, wave 2, or persistent food insecurity in both waves.			
Weight-for-age Z-score		No statistically significant association between weight-for-age Z-scores at wave 2 and food insecurity among adults measured at wave 1, wave 2, or persistent food insecurity in both waves.			
Health Status (Mother reported)		Children in households with food insecurity among adults at wave 2 had poorer health (0.17 points lower) at wave 2. In separate analyses of boys and girls, the effect on boys' health was not statisti cally significant, but girls in food insecure households had poorer health (0.19 points lower).		Counterintuitive finding that food insecurity among adults at wave 2 affected child's health status, but food insecurity at both wave 1 and at wave 2 did not significantly affect health status.	
		Food insecurity among adults at wave 1 was not significantly associated with child health status at wave 2. Food insecurity at both waves was not associated with health status at wave 2.			
Iron deficiency anemia	Children ages 0-36 months	1.98 times more likely for children in households with very low food security	Children's Health-Watch (formerly C-SNAP)		Park et al., 2009
Iron deficiency		No statistically significant association.			

Appendix Table A. (Continued)

Condition studied	Population	Finding	Data[1]	Comments	Citation
Attachment and mental proficiency	Children age 9 months and 24 months	Children in food insecure households at 9 months more likely to have insecure child attachment at 24 months and less advanced mental proficiency through indirect pathways operating through maternal depression and in turn parenting practices.	ECLS-B		Zaslow et al., 2009
Weight and BMI	Children in first, third, and fifth grade	Weak, nonsignificant negative association with food insecurity in current period (for boys, girls, and combined).	ECLS-K	Extensively speci-fied dynamic model controlled for weight in previous period (kindergarten, first, and third grade).	Bhargava et al., 2008
Developmental risk (parent reported concerns about child's development in: ex- pressive and receptive language, fine and gross motor, behavior, social/emotional, self-help, and school)	Children ages 4-36 months	1.76 times as likely for children in food-insecure households	Children's Health-Watch (formerly C-SNAP)		Rose-Jacobs et al., 2008

Condition studied	Population	Finding	Data[1]	Comments	Citation
General health (parent reported)	Children ages 9 and 24 months	Poor or fair health (versus excellent or good) more likely in food-insecure house holds. Main pathway is through parental depression, direct effect marginally significant (p=.09), not through measured parenting or feeding practices.	ECLS-B	Could be biased by measurement artifact of parental depression, leading to upward bias on measured food insecurity and children's poor health.	Bronte-Tinkew et al., 2007
Weight for length (over-weight)	Children ages 9 and 24 months	Higher weight for length in food-insecure households. Pathway is through parent ing practices and infant feeding practices (mainly a measure of breastfeeding).		Structural model may be problematic. Food insecurity associ-ated with better infant feeding practices and marginally significant (p=.07).	
Length for age	Children ages 9 and 24 months	No significant association with food insecurity or mediating variables.			
Iron deficiency anemia	Children ages 7-36 months	2.5 times more likely in households with food insecurity among children.	Children's Health-Watch (formerly C-SNAP)	Sample was small. Should be repeated with larger sample.	Skalicky et al., 2006
Anemia without iron deficiency	Children ages 7-36 months	1.6 times more likely in households with food insecurity among children, but not statistically significant.			

Appendix Table A. (Continued)

Condition studied	Population	Finding	Data[1]	Comments	Citation
Behavioral problems (problem in one or more of three domains: aggressive, anxious/ depressed, inattention/ hyperactivity)	Children age 3	Significant behavioral problems 1.6 times more likely in households with marginal food security among adults and 2.1 times more likely in households with food-insecure adults. Similar and statistically significant associations with each problem domain individually.	Fragile Families	Strong results in a large sample. In addition to demographic and economic con-trols, mother's mental health (which could be a confounding measurement factor) was controlled.	Whitaker et al., 2006
Physical function (a subscale of the Pediatric Health- Related Quality of Life measure)	Children ages 3-17	Physical function of children in food-insecure households 3.3 points lower (87.4 versus 90.7 mean for children in food-secure households); association was strongest for ages 3-8, weaker and not statistically significant for ages 9-11, and near zero for ages 12-17.	Delta NIRI		Casey et al., 2005
Psychosocial func tion (a subscale of the Pediatric Health- Related Quality of Life measure)		Psychosocial function of children in food-insecure households 3.6 points lower (77.1 versus 80.7 in food-secure households); association was strongest for ages 12-17, weaker and not statistically significant for ages 3-8, and near zero for ages 9-11.			

Condition studied	Population	Finding	Data[1]	Comments	Citation
Change in BMI and weight from kindergarten to third grade	Girls in third grade	Higher in households with marginal food security or insecurity at kindergarten age; higher in households with marginal food security or insecurity in both kindergarten and third grade.	ECLS-K		Jyoti et al., 2005
	Boys in third grade	No statistically significant association.			
Change in math score from kindergarten to third grade	Girls and boys in third grade	Lower in households marginally food secure or food insecure in kindergarten than in households food secure in both kindergarten and third grade.			
Change in reading score from kindergarten to third grade	Girls in third grade	Lower in households marginally food secure or food insecure in third grade (or in both kindergarten and third grade) than in households food secure in both periods.			
	Boys in third grade	No statistically significant association.			
Change in social skills as assessed by teachers in kindergarten and third grade	Girls in third grade	Greater improvement in households that transitioned from marginally food secure or food insecure in kindergarten to food secure in third grade than in households food secure in both periods.			
	Boys in third grade	Smaller improvement (opposite of girls) in households that transitioned from marginally food secure or food insecure in kindergarten to food secure in third grade than in households food secure in both periods.		Unexpected finding, and unexpected that boys and girls have opposite patterns.	

Appendix Table A. (Continued)

Condition studied	Population	Finding	Data[1]	Comments	Citation
Externalizing behavior problems	Children ages 3-5	Positively associated with food hardship. The relationship is mediated by parental characteristics (parental stress, warmth, and depression).	Illinois Family Study[3]		Slack and Yoo, 2005
	Children ages 6-12	No statistically significant association.			
Internalizing behavior problems	Children ages 3-5	Positively associated with food hardship. The relationship is mediated by parental characteristics (parental stress, warmth, and depression).			
	Children ages 6-12	Positively associated with food hardship. The relationship is mediated by parental characteristics (parental stress, warmth, and depression).			
Health status (reported by caregiver)	Children ages 0-36 months	Fair or poor health (versus excellent or good) nearly twice as likely in food-insecure households; no dose-response pattern observed.	Children's Health-Watch (formerly C-SNAP)		Cook et al., 2004
Hospitalization since birth		30 percent more likely in food-insecure households; dose response: 2.3 times more likely in households with very low food security.			
Hospital admission on day of interview		Not statistically significant; weak negative association in sample.			
At risk for growth problems (either low weight for age or weight for height)		Not statistically significant; weak positive association in sample.			

Condition studied	Population	Finding	Data[1]	Comments	Citation
Educational achievement—math score in fall of kindergarten year	Children in kindergarten	Lower by a half-point (mean math score was 19 points) in marginally secure and food-insecure households. Some dose response: score 1 point lower in households with very low food security.	ECLS-K		Winicki and Jemison, 2003
Educational achievement—gain in math score from fall to spring of kindergarten year		Lower by 0.4 points (mean gain in math score was 8 points) in marginally secure or food-insecure households; no dose-response pattern.			
Physical growth— height, weight, BMI, and changes in these from fall to spring		Not statistically significant; associations in the sample weak and inconsistent.			
Depressive disorder and suicidal symptoms	Children ages 15-16	Adolescents in food insufficient house-holds much more likely to have depressive disorder and suicidal symptoms.	NHANES III		Alaimo et al., 2002
Chronic health condition count	Preschool children	Significantly higher in households with moderate child hunger.	Worcester, MA survey of homeless and low-income, housed mothers and children		Weinreb et al., 2002
	School-age children	Significantly higher in households with severe child hunger (measured by CCHIP items).[4]			
Internalizing behavior problems (based on Child Behavior Checklist)	Preschool and school-age children	Significantly higher in households with severe child hunger, associations positive but weaker and not statistically significant with moderate child hunger.			
Anxiety/depression (based on Child Behavior Checklist)	School-age children	Significantly higher in households with severe child hunger.			
Academic achievement (based on Wechsler Individual Achievement Test Screener)	School-age children	No statistically significant association.			

Appendix Table A. (Continued)

Condition studied	Population	Finding	Data[1]	Comments	Citation
Risk of overweight (weight-for-age higher than 85th percentile on CDC growth chart)	Girls ages 2-7	Significantly lower in food insufficient households.	NHANES III		Alaimo et al., 2001b
	Boys ages 2-7	No statistically significant association.			
	Boys ages 8-16	No statistically significant association.			
	White non-Hispanic girls ages 8-16	No statistically significant association.			
	Black non-Hispanic girls ages 8-16	No statistically significant association.			
	Mexican-American girls ages 8-16	Significantly higher in food insufficient households.			
Fair or poor health status (versus excellent or good)	Children ages 1-5	49 percent more likely in food insufficient households.	NHANES III		Alaimo et al., 2001
	Children ages 6-16	58 percent more likely in food insufficient households.			
Frequent stomach aches	Children ages 4-5	3 times as likely in food insufficient households.			
	Children ages 6-16	88 percent more likely in food insufficient households.			
Frequent headaches	Children ages 4-5	2.5 times as likely in food insufficient households.			
	Children ages 6-16	67 percent more likely in food insufficient households.			
Number of colds in previous 12 months	Children ages 1-5	57 percent more likely in food insufficient households.			
	Children ages 6-16	Moderately strong positive association in the sample, but not statistically significant.			
Number of ear infections in lifetime	Children ages 1-5	Association weakly positive in sample, but not statistically significant.			

Condition studied	Population	Finding	Data[1]	Comments	Citation
	Children ages 6-16	Association weakly positive in sample, but not statistically significant.			
Iron deficiency	Children ages 1-5	Association negative (opposite of expected) in sample, but not statistically significant.			
	Children ages 6-16	Association negative (opposite of expected) in sample, but not statistically significant.			
Restrictive impairment (ages 1-5, prevented usual activity; ages 6-16, prevented school attendance)	Children ages 1-5	Association positive in sample, but not statistically significant.			
	Children ages 6-16	Association positive in sample, but not statistically significant.			
Cognitive development (two subtests of Weschler Intelligence Scale for Children- Revised)	Children ages 6-11	No statistically significant association.	NHANES III		Alaimo et al., 2001a
	Children ages 12-16	No statistically significant association.			
Academic development (two subtests of Wide Range Achievement Test-Revised, repeated grade, days absent)	Children ages 6-11	Lower arithmetic score and more likely to have repeated a grade in food insufficient households.			
	Children ages 12-16	No statistically significant association. Associations in sample weak and inconsistent.			
Psychosocial development (school absence, professional help for mental health, school suspension, number of good friends, trouble getting along with other children, shyness or slow to make friends)	Children ages 6-11	Child in food insufficient households 89 percent more likely to have seen psychologist or other mental health profes- sional because of an emotional, mental, or behavioral problem.			
	Children ages 6-11	Positive association with "difficulty getting along with others" in sample, but not statistically significant.			

Appendix Table A. (Continued)

Condition studied	Population	Finding	Data[1]	Comments	Citation
	Children ages 12-16	Child in food-insufficient households 82 percent more likely to have seen psychologist or other mental health professional because of an emotional, mental, or behavioral problem, 95 percent more likely to have been suspended, 74 percent more likely to have difficulty getting along with others.			
Psychosocial dysfunction (based on Pediatric Symptom Checklist)	Children ages 6-12	Significantly more likely in households with hungry children. Aggression and anxiety components particularly strongly associated with hunger.	CCHIP[5] Pittsburgh area		Kleinman et al., 1998

BMI=Body mass index.

[1]Data source abbreviations: ECLS-B, Early Childhood Longitudinal Study-Birth Cohort (National Center for Education Statistics); ECLS-K, Early Childhood Longitudinal Study-Kindergarten Cohort (National Center for Education Statistics); C-SNAP, Children's Sentinel Nutrition Assessment Program, renamed Children's Healthwatch in 2009; Delta NIRI, Lower Mississippi Delta Nutrition Intervention Research Initiative (consortium of USDA's Agriculture Research Service, several land-grant universities, and other institutions in the region); Fragile Families, The Fragile Families and Child Wellbeing Study (Princeton University); NHANES III, National Health and Nutrition Examination Survey III (National Center for Health Statistics); NLSCY, National (Canadian) Longitudinal Survey of Children and Youth (Statistics Canada and Human Resources and Skills Development Canada)

[2]The Kirkpatrick et al. (2010) study determined child's hunger status based on a "yes" response by the person most knowledgeable of child's food intake to the question, "Has [the child] ever experienced being hungry because the family has run out of food or money to buy food?"

[3]The Slack and Yoo (2005) study determined food hardship by summing parental responses to four items derived from the child items of USDA's Household Food Security scale.

[4]The Weinreb et al. (2002) study used a methodology developed by the Community Childhood Hunger Identification Project (CCHIP). The measure is closely related to the Children's Food Security Scale based on the HFSSM and includes many of the same items.

Based on the number of food insecure conditions reported, households are classified as no hunger, adult or moderate child hunger, or severe child hunger.

[5]The Kleinman et al. (1998) study used data from a Community Childhood Hunger Identification Project (CCHIP) survey in low-income areas of Pittsburgh and surrounding Allegheny County. Children's food security status was measured by the same eight questions as in Weinreb et al. (2002; see footnote 4), but categories were labeled as not hungry, at risk for hunger, or hungry.

APPENDIX B: INCIDENCE OF FOOD INSECURITY IN SELECTED SUBPOPULATIONS, AVERAGE 2010-11

Appendix B table provides the statistics presented graphically in the main body of the report on food insecurity in households with children by selected household characteristics. The corresponding statistics for the broader category of food insecurity also are included for households with food insecurity among either adults or children.

For example, out of a total of 25.6 million married-couple households with children, about 3.5 million were food insecure, comprising 13.9 percent of all married-couple households with children and 44.4 percent of all food-insecure households with children. Children and adults were food insecure in about 1.6 million married-couple households (a subset of the 3.5 million that were food insecure), comprising 6.4 percent of married-couple households with children and 42.2 percent of all households with food insecurity among children. Children experienced very low food security at times during the year in 167,000 married-couple households, comprising 0.7 percent of married-couple households with children and 44.0 percent of all households with very low food security among children. These households with very low food security among children represent a more severely food-insecure subset of the households with food insecurity among children.

Appendix Table B. Prevalence and distribution of food insecurity in households with children, by selected household characteristics, 2010-11 average

Characteristic	All food security statuses	Food-insecure households (food insecurity among adults or children)			Households with food insecurity among children (low or very low food security among children)			Households with very low food security among children		
	Number	Number	Prevalence	Share	Number	Prevalence	Share	Number	Prevalence	Share
	1,000	*1,000*	*— Percent —*		*1,000*	*— Percent —*		*1,000*	*— Percent —*	
All households with children	39,111	7,980	20.4	100.0	3,861	9.9	100.0	380	1.0	100.0
Household composition:										
Married-couple household	25,575	3,546	13.9	44.4	1,629	6.4	42.2	167	0.7	44.0
Cohabiting household	2,790	805	28.8	10.1	342	12.3	8.9	29	1.0	7.5
Single female-headed household	8,528	3,112	36.5	39.0	1,635	19.2	42.3	165	1.9	43.5
Single male-headed household	1,896	459	24.2	5.7	221	11.7	5.7	16	0.8	4.2
Other household with children	322	58	18.1	0.7	34	10.5	0.9	3	0.9	0.8
Race and Hispanic ethnicity:[1]										
White non-Hispanic	23,453	3,509	15.0	44.0	1,498	6.4	38.8	112	0.5	29.4
Black non-Hispanic	5,416	1,685	31.1	21.1	838	15.5	21.7	104	1.9	27.3
Hispanic[2]	7,455	2,344	31.4	29.4	1,280	17.2	33.2	136	1.8	35.7
Other non-Hispanic	2,787	443	15.9	5.5	245	8.8	6.3	29	1.0	7.6
Annual household income:										
Below Federal poverty line[3]	7,067	3,166	44.8	39.7	1,700	24.1	44.0	196	2.8	51.7
100-130 percent of poverty line	2,468	906	36.7	11.3	422	17.1	10.9	41	1.7	10.9
130-185 percent of poverty line	3,615	1,140	31.5	14.3	558	15.4	14.5	45	1.2	11.9
Above 185 percent of poverty line	19,021	1,631	8.6	20.4	647	3.4	16.8	51	0.3	13.5
Income not reported	6,940	1,138	16.4	14.3	534	7.7	13.8	46	0.7	12.1
Residence relative to Metropolitan Statistical Area (MSA):										
In principal city of MSA[4]	10,409	2,548	24.5	31.9	1,274	12.2	33.0	131	1.3	34.6

Characteristic	All food security statuses	Food-insecure households (food insecurity among adults or children)			Households with food insecurity among children (low or very low food security among children)			Households with very low food security among children		
	Number	Number	Prevalence	Share	Number	Prevalence	Share	Number	Prevalence	Share
	1,000	*1,000*	*— Percent —*		*1,000*	*— Percent —*		*1,000*	*— Percent —*	
In suburbs or outlying areas of MSA[5]	17,199	3,009	17.5	37.7	1,429	8.3	37.0	146	0.9	38.5
In MSA, specific location not identified	5,496	1,135	20.7	14.2	553	10.1	14.3	52	0.9	13.6
Not in MSA (i.e., nonmetropolitan)	6,007	1,288	21.4	16.1	605	10.1	15.7	50	0.8	13.3
Census Region:										
Northeast	6,761	1,230	18.2	15.4	578	8.5	15.0	51	0.8	13.3
Midwest	8,311	1,469	17.7	18.4	670	8.1	17.3	63	0.8	16.7
South	14,696	3,193	21.7	40.0	1,567	10.7	40.6	181	1.2	47.6
West	9,343	2,089	22.4	26.2	1,046	11.2	27.1	85	0.9	22.4
Employment and labor force status of adults:										
One or more employed full-time	32,247	5,073	15.7	63.6	2,301	7.1	59.6	219	0.7	57.6
Part-time, no full-time	2,767	1,111	40.2	13.9	593	21.4	15.4	51	1.8	13.4
Unemployed looking for work, none employed	1,840	861	46.8	10.8	470	25.5	12.2	53	2.9	13.8
Disabled, none in labor force	849	453	53.3	5.7	249	29.4	6.5	26	3.1	6.9
None in labor force for reasons other than disability	1,408	483	34.3	6.1	248	17.6	6.4	31	2.2	8.3
Disability status of adults in household:										
Not in labor force due to disability	2,483	1,005	40.5	12.6	509	20.5	13.2	56	2.2	14.7
Other reported disability (ages 18-64)[6]	1,879	691	36.8	8.7	335	17.8	8.7	45	2.4	11.8
No working-age adult with disability	34,749	6,284	18.1	78.7	3,017	8.7	78.1	279	0.8	73.5
Education of most highly educated adult:										
Less than high school	2,706	1,147	42.4	14.4	655	24.2	17.0	77	2.8	20.1
Completed high school (or GED)	8,525	2,525	29.6	31.6	1,238	14.5	32.1	99	1.2	26.0
Some college (including 2-year degree)	12,515	3,069	24.5	38.5	1,406	11.2	36.4	149	1.2	39.1

Appendix Table B. (Continued)

Characteristic	All food security statuses	Food-insecure households (food insecurity among adults or children)			Households with food insecurity among children (low or very low food security among children)			Households with very low food security among children		
	Number	Number	Prevalence	Share	Number	Prevalence	Share	Number	Prevalence	Share
	1,000	*1,000*	*— Percent —*		*1,000*	*— Percent —*		*1,000*	*— Percent —*	
Four-year degree or higher	15,366	1,241	8.1	15.5	564	3.7	14.6	56	0.4	14.8
Age of oldest child in the household:										
0-4 years	7,630	1,403	18.4	17.6	452	5.9	11.7	33	0.4	8.6
5-8 years	7,075	1,436	20.3	18.0	680	9.6	17.6	54	0.8	14.2
9-12 years	8,353	1,819	21.8	22.8	938	11.2	24.3	78	0.9	20.5
13-15 years	8,374	1,792	21.4	22.5	952	11.4	24.7	103	1.2	27.2
16-17 years	7,678	1,529	19.9	19.2	840	10.9	21.8	112	1.5	29.5
Number of children in the household:										
1 child	16,853	3,158	18.7	39.6	1,311	7.8	34.0	115	0.7	30.3
2 children	14,145	2,656	18.8	33.3	1,301	9.2	33.7	122	0.9	32.1
3 or more children	8,113	2,166	26.7	27.1	1,249	15.4	32.3	143	1.8	37.6

Notes: For each characteristic and food security status, "prevalence" means the number of households with the specified food security status and the specified characteristic as a percentage of all households with the specified characteristic. "Share" means the number of households with the specified food security status and the specified characteristic as a percentage of all households with the specified food security status. For example, 13.9 percent of married-couple households were food insecure and married-couple households made up 44.4 percent of all food-insecure households.

[1]Race and Hispanic ethnicity refers to that of the household reference person (i.e., the person in whose name the residence is owned or rented). If residence is jointly owned or rented, any of the owners or lessees may be designated reference person.

[2]Hispanics may be of any race.

[3]The Federal poverty line for a family of two adults and two children in 2011 was an annual income of $22,811. [4]Households within incorporated areas of the largest cities in each metropolitan area.

[5]Households in counties (or townships in New England) that are densely populated and linked to principal cities of the MSA by daily commuting patterns.

[6]Other reported disabilities include hearing, vision, mental, physical, self-care, and going-outside-home disabilities. Working-age adults with these disabilities were not reported to be out of the labor force due to disability.

Source: USDA, Economic Research Service calculations based on Current Population Survey Food Security Supplement data.

End Notes

[1] This specification of the threshold for low food security among children (reports of two or more food-insecure indicators) was adopted by USDA to be conceptually consistent with the corresponding threshold for adult/household food insecurity. For the adult and household scales, the threshold for food insecurity corresponds with the severity of not being able to afford balanced meals. For the child scale, the threshold corresponds with the severity of not being able to afford to feed children balanced meals. Low food security among children is identified in the Current Population Survey Food Security Supplement (CPS-FSS) data, beginning with December 2006 data, and USDA first published statistics on the category in 2009, using data from 2006-07 (Nord, 2009).

[2] Prior to the development of the food security measures, the National Health and Nutrition Examination Survey (NHANES) and the Continuing Study of Food Intake by Individuals (CSFII) assessed the adequacy of households' food access using a single question. Respondents were asked which of three statements best described the food eaten in their household:

- "We always have enough to eat."
- "Sometimes we don't have enough to eat."
- "Often we don't have enough to eat."

Households were classified as food sufficient if they reported that they always had enough to eat and food insufficient if they reported that they sometimes or often did not have enough to eat.

[3] The Federal poverty line for a family of two adults and two children in 2011 was an annual income of $22,811; 185 percent of the poverty line for that family was $42,200.

[4] In 2011, the poverty rate for children under age 18 was just under 22 percent (DeNavas-Walt et al., 2012). In 2011, the Federal poverty line was $22,811 for a family of four with two adults and two children.

[5] These percentages may be higher, depending on the income of those households that did not report income.

[6] Eligibility for Federal food and nutrition assistance programs is based on an income cutoff that differs across programs and other criteria that differ across States for some programs. Eligibility for programs is determined by current monthly income, whereas income reported here is annual income.

[7] Working-age adults with "other reported disabilities" were reported as having a vision, hearing, mental, physical, self-care, or going-outside-home disability but were not identified as being unable to work due to disability. For more detailed information on this classification, see Coleman-Jensen and Nord, 2013.

[8] This is the first ERS report to provide separate food security statistics for households with a cohabiting couple. The category comprises households in which an adult member was identified as an unmarried partner of the household reference person. In previous reports, these households were classified as single female-headed households, single male-headed households, or other households with children.

[9] Multivariate analysis (not shown) confirms that this association is largely independent of the number of children in the household and the greater food needs of older children.

[10] The food security survey identifies Metropolitan Statistical Areas (MSAs) and principal cities within them in accordance with standards delineated in 2003 by the Office of Management and Budget, based on revised standards developed by the U.S. Census Bureau in

collaboration with other Federal agencies. Principal cities include the incorporated areas of the largest city in each MSA and other cities in the MSAs that meet specified criteria based on population size and commuting patterns.

[11] Statistics on very low food security among children are not presented by program participation categories because of inadequate sample sizes in some categories. Numbers of households are not reported because about 18 percent of households with children do not report income. Most such households are not asked about participation in food and nutrition assistance programs. The omission of those households would result in understating the numbers of households in the various participation categories. Participation in food and nutrition assistance programs is also underreported in the CPS-FSS, which would further distort estimated numbers of participants.

[12] Some households with average annual incomes above the income eligibility limit may have been eligible for food assistance if their monthly income was within the income eligibility limits.

[13] In spite of sizable denominators (all households with children interviewed) in all States, the number of interviewed households with very low food security among children was less than 10 in several States and as few as 3 in some. Estimates based on such small numerators are unreliable because an error in measurement, or the chance selection or omission of a single household in the sample, could change the estimate by a large proportion.

[14] Some households with average annual incomes above the eligibility thresholds may have had monthly incomes that qualified them for food assistance in some months of the year.

In: Food Insecurity in U.S. Households ... ISBN: 978-1-62948-015-2
Editor: Dustin C. Bertram

Chapter 2

CHILD NUTRITION AND WIC PROGRAMS: A BRIEF OVERVIEW

Joe Richardson

SUMMARY

Federally supported child nutrition programs and initiatives, along with the Special Supplemental Nutrition Program for Women, Infants, and Children (the WIC program) reach more than 40 million children and some 2 million lower-income pregnant/post-partum women. In FY2007, federal spending on these programs totaled over $19 billion.

The basic goals of federal child nutrition programs are to improve children's nutrition, increase lower-income children's access to nutritious meals and snacks, and help support the agricultural economy. Child nutrition programs are "entitlements." Federal cash funding and commodity support is "guaranteed" to schools and other providers based on the number of meals/snacks served, who is served (e.g., free meals for poor children get higher subsidies), and legislatively established (and inflation-indexed) per-meal subsidy rates. On the other hand, the WIC program is a "discretionary" grant program where specific annual appropriations to pay for benefits and nutrition services and administration are distributed by formula.

In addition to the WIC program (and its ancillary farmers' market program), the child nutrition programs covered in this report include the School Lunch and Breakfast programs (providing federal subsidies for meals served in schools), day-care, summer and other outside-of-school programs assisting sponsors in providing meals/snacks, and payments to states covering administrative oversight costs, expenses for a Fresh Fruit and Vegetable program, the Special Milk program, and various support activities (e.g., various administrative oversight and nutrition education activities).

The underlying laws covering child nutrition and WIC programs were last reauthorized in 2004 in the Child Nutrition and WIC Reauthorization Act (P.L. 108-265). The next reauthorization is scheduled for 2009. The Administration's FY2010 budget calls for increased funding of approximately $1 billion a year for child nutrition programs (for "program reforms aimed at improving program access, enhancing the nutritional quality of school meals, expanding nutrition research and evaluation, and improving program oversight").

BACKGROUND

Child nutrition programs and the WIC program provide cash, commodity, and other assistance (including funds for nutrition services and food packages in the WIC program and technical assistance and administrative cost aid in child nutrition programs) under three major federal laws: the Richard B. Russell National School Lunch Act (originally enacted as the National School Lunch Act in 1946), the Child Nutrition Act (originally enacted in 1966), and Section 32 of the Act of August 24, 1935 (7 U.S.C. 612c). The Agriculture Department's Food and Nutrition Service (FNS) administers the programs at the federal level; most funding is included in the annual Agriculture Department appropriations laws; and congressional jurisdiction over the underlying three laws is exercised by the Senate Agriculture, Nutrition, and Forestry Committee; the House Education and Labor Committee; and, to a limited extent (relating to commodity assistance and Section 32 issues), the House Agriculture Committee. Congress periodically reviews and reauthorizes expiring authorities under these laws. The most recent reauthorization was in 2004 (P.L. 108-265); the next reauthorization is scheduled for 2009.

Child nutrition and WIC programs are operated by a wide variety of local public and private providers, and the degree of direct state involvement varies by program and state - e.g., in the WIC program, state health agencies exercise substantial control; in the school meal programs, local educational agencies (LEAs) and local "school food authorities" most often have the major role; in a very few instances, the federal government (FNS) takes the place of state agencies (for example, where a state has chosen not to operate a specific program or where there is a state prohibition on aiding private schools). At the state level, education, health, social services, and agriculture departments all have roles; at a minimum, they are responsible for approving and overseeing local providers such as schools, summer program sponsors, and child care centers and day care homes, as well as making sure they receive the federal support they are due. At the local level, program benefits are provided to more than 40 million children and infants, and some 2 million lower-income pregnant and post-partum women, through some 100,000 public and private schools and residential child care institutions, about 200,000 child care centers and family day care homes, approximately 30,000 summer program sites, and (in the case of the WIC program) about 10,000 local health care clinics/sites operated by nearly 2,000 health agencies.

All programs are available in the 50 states and the District of Columbia. Virtually all operate in Puerto Rico, Guam, and the Virgin Islands (and, in differing versions, in the Northern Marianas and American Samoa), and there are no restrictions on eligibility related to citizenship or legal residence status. In addition, WIC-like benefits are available to overseas military personnel, and Defense Department overseas dependents' schools participate in the school meal programs.

In the meal service programs like the School Lunch and Breakfast programs, summer programs, and assistance for child care centers and day care homes, federal aid is in the form of legislatively set subsidies ("reimbursements") paid for each meal/snack served that meets federal nutrition guidelines. Most subsidies are cash payments to schools or other providers, but about 10% of the total value of all aid is in the form of federally donated food commodities. Although all meals/snacks served by participating providers are subsidized, those served free or at a reduced price to lower-income children are supported at higher rates. All federal meal/snack subsidy rates are indexed annually (each July) for inflation, as are the income standards of eligibility for free and reduced-price meals/snacks. However federal subsidies do not necessarily cover the full cost of the meals and snacks offered by providers, and states and localities contribute to cover program costs—as do children's families (by paying charges for nonfree or reduced-price meals/snacks). Required nonfederal cost sharing is relatively minimal - states must expend at least an amount totaling some $200 million a year nationally in order to receive federal school lunch funds. Federal per-meal/snack child nutrition subsidies may cover local providers' administrative/operating costs, but separate direct federal payments for administrative/operating costs are limited to expense grants to state oversight agencies, a small set-aside of funds for state audits of child care sponsors, and special administrative payments to sponsors of summer programs and family day care homes. Under the WIC program, federal appropriations pay the cost of specifically tailored food packages and include legislatively set amounts for costs of administrative and nutrition services.

SCHOOL LUNCH AND SCHOOL BREAKFAST PROGRAMS

The School Lunch and School Breakfast programs provide federal cash and commodity support for meals meeting minimum federally set nutrition standards. The meals are served by public and private nonprofit elementary and secondary schools and residential child care institutions (RCCIs) that opt to enroll and guarantee to offer free or reduced price meals to eligible low income children. Both programs are "entitlement" programs, and both subsidize participating schools and RCCIs for all meals served that meet federal nutrition standards at specific, inflation- indexed rates for each meal; food items not served as part of a meal meeting nutrition standards (e.g., a la carte offerings) are not eligible for subsidies.

Each program has a three-tiered system for cash per meal federal reimbursements to schools and RCCIs.

1. It allows children to receive free meals if they have family income below 130% of the federal poverty guidelines ($27,580 for a four-person family in the 2008- 2009 school year); these meals receive the highest subsidy rate.
2. Children may receive reduced price meals (no more than 40 cents for a lunch or 30 cents for a breakfast) if their family income is between 130% and 185% of the poverty guidelines (between $27,580 and $39,220 for a four-person family in the 2008-2009 school year); these meals receive a subsidy rate either 40 cents (for lunches) or 30 cents (for breakfasts) below the free meal rate.
3. A small per meal subsidy is provided for "full-price" or "paid" meals (the price is set by the school or RCCI) served to children whose families do not apply, or whose family income does not qualify them, for free or reduced price meals.

Children in Temporary Assistance for Needy Families (TANF) programs and the Supplemental Nutrition Assistance Program (the SNAP, formerly the Food Stamp program) may automatically qualify for free school meals. Information across these programs can be shared to facilitate this through "direct certification" and other means.

Table 1. School Lunch Program Participation and Federal Costs, Selected Fiscal Years 1980-2007 (in millions)

	Average Daily Participation[a]				Federal costs	
	Free meals	Reduced-price meals	Full-price meals[b]	Total[c]	Current Dollars[d]	Constant 2007 Dollars[e]
1980	10.0	1.9	14.7	26.6	$3,044.9	$7,813.2
1985	9.9	1.6	12.1	23.6	3,034.4	5,841.2
1990	9.8	1.7	12.6	24.1	3,677.1	5,865.0
1992	11.2	1.7	11.7	24.6	4,439.2	6,543.4
1994	12.2	1.8	11.3	25.3	4,919.9	6,858.3
1996	12.6	2.0	11.3	25.9	5,308.7	7,002.2
1998	13.0	2.2	11.4	26.6	5,744.1	7,260.5
2000	13.0	2.5	11.9	27.3	6,099.5	7,331.6
2001	12.9	2.6	12.0	27.5	6,414.5	7,466.5
2002	13.3	2.6	12.0	28.0	6,770.2	7,772.2
2003	13.7	2.7	11.9	28.4	7,037.5	7,889.0
2004	14.1	2.8	12.0	29.0	7,425.5	8,138.3
2005	14.6	2.9	12.2	29.6	7,879.3	8,359.9
2006	14.8	2.9	12.4	30.1	8,162.1	8,349.8
2007	14.9	3.0	12.6	30.5	8,726.5	8,726.5

Source: Compiled by the Congressional Research Service (CRS) based on data from the U.S. Department of Agriculture, Food and Nutrition Service.

a. In order to reflect participation for the actual school year (September through May), these estimates are based on 9 month averages of October through May, plus September, rather than averages of the 12 months of the fiscal year (October through September).

b. The federal government provides a small subsidy for these meals.

c. Details may not sum to total because of rounding.

d. Includes cash payments and the value of “entitlement” commodities; does not include the value of “bonus” commodities provided at the Agriculture Department’s discretion.

e. Constant dollars were calculated using the fiscal year CPI-U.

The School Lunch Program subsidizes lunches (5.1 billion in FY2007) to children in about 6,000 RCCIs and almost all schools (95,000). During FY2007, average daily participation was 30.5 million students (61% of the 50 million children enrolled in participating schools and RCCIs); of these, 49% received free lunches, and 10% ate reduced-price lunches (Table 1). The remainder were served full-price (but still subsidized) meals. More than 90% of federal funding is used to subsidize free and reduced-price lunches served to low income children. For the 2008-2009 school year, inflation-indexed per lunch federal subsidies (cash payments, plus a required, and inflation-indexed, 21 cents a meal in "entitlement" commodity support) range from 45 cents for full price lunches to $2.78 and $2.38 for free and reduced price lunches, respectively. FY2007 federal school lunch costs (including commodity assistance) totaled some $8.7 billion (Table 1).

The School Breakfast program serves fewer students than does the School Lunch program; about 1.7 billion breakfasts in 80,000 schools (and 6,000 RCCIs) were subsidized in FY2007. Average daily participation was 10.1 million children (23% of the 43 million students enrolled in participating schools and RCCIs). Unlike the School Lunch program, the great majority received free or reduced price meals: 70% received free meals, and 10% purchased reduced price meals. In the 2008-2009 school year, inflation-indexed per breakfast federal subsidies (cash only) range from 25 cents for full price meals to $1.40 and $1.10 for free and reduced price breakfasts, respectively. FY2007 federal school breakfast funding totaled about $2.2 billion (Table 2).

In addition to federal cash subsidies, participating schools receive donations of federally acquired food commodities. Schools are “entitled” to a specific, inflation-indexed value of federally provided commodities for each lunch they serve (20.75 cents a meal for the 2008-2009 school year); they also may receive “bonus” commodities acquired by the Agriculture Department in support of the farm economy. In recent years, the value of federal commodity aid to schools has totaled well over $1 billion a year, and, by law, commodity assistance must represent at least 12% of the total value (cash + commodities) of aid given under the School Lunch program. Cash and commodity support to participating schools is based on the number and type of meals served (e.g., lunch or breakfast, free or full price). However, once the aid is received by the school, it is used to support the overall school meal service budget, as determined appropriate by the school.

Table 2. School Breakfast Program Participation and Federal Costs, Selected Fiscal Years 1980-2007 (in millions)

	Average Daily Participation[a]				Federal Costs	
	Free meals	Reducedprice meals	Full-price meals[b]	Total[c]	Current dollars[d]	Constant 2007 Dollars[e]
1980	2.8	0.2	0.6	3.6	$287.8	$738.5
1985	2.9	0.2	0.4	3.4	379.3	730.2
1990	3.3	0.2	0.5	4.0	596.2	950.9
1992	4.0	0.2	0.6	4.9	786.5	1,159.3
1994	4.8	0.3	0.7	5.8	959.0	1,336.8
1996	5.3	0.4	0.9	6.6	1,118.7	1,475.6
1998	5.6	0.5	1.0	7.1	1,272.2	1,608.1
2000	5.7	0.6	1.2	7.5	1,393.3	1,674.7
2001	5.8	0.7	1.3	7.8	1,450.1	1,689.4
2002	6.0	0.7	1.4	8.1	1,566.7	1,798.6
2003	6.2	0.7	1.5	8.4	1,651.8	1,851.7
2004	6.5	0.8	1.6	8.9	1,775.7	1,946.2
2005	6.8	0.9	1.7	9.4	1,927.2	2,044.8
2006	7.0	0.9	1.9	9.8	2,042.9	2,089.9
2007	7.1	1.0	2.0	10.1	2,163.8	2,163.8

Source: Compiled by the Congressional Research Service (CRS) based on data from the U.S. Department of Agriculture, Food and Nutrition Service.

a. In order to reflect participation for the actual school year (September through May), these estimates are based on 9 month averages of October through May, plus September, rather than averages of the 12 months of the fiscal year (October through September).

b. The federal government provides a small subsidy for these meals.

c. Details may not sum to total because of rounding.

d. Does not include the value of any federally donated commodities.

e. Note – Constant dollars were calculated using the fiscal year CPI-U.

SPECIAL SUPPLEMENTAL NUTRITION PROGRAM FOR WOMEN, INFANTS, AND CHILDREN (THE WIC PROGRAM)

The WIC Program provides food assistance, nutrition risk screening, and related services (e.g., nutrition education and breastfeeding support, medical care referral) to low-income pregnant and postpartum women and their infants, as well as to children up to age 5 from low-income families. Participants in the program generally must have family income at or below 185% of poverty, and must be judged to be nutritionally at risk. Nutrition risk is defined as detectable abnormal nutritional conditions; documented nutritionally related medical conditions; health impairing dietary deficiencies; or conditions that predispose people to inadequate nutrition or nutritionally related medical problems. Most income-eligible applicants meet the WIC program's nutrition risk criteria.

Beneficiaries of the WIC Program receive monthly vouchers for the purchase of a "package" of specifically prescribed food items in participating retail stores (or, in some cases, actual monthly food packages of supplemental foods directly provided by state agencies). The range of permissible food items is set by federal regulation, although administering state agencies have some latitude in how federal standards are carried out (e.g., specifying "store" brands, decisions as to what types of infant formula are covered, what food may be provided for those with special dietary needs). Among the items that may be included are milk, cheese, eggs, infant formula, cereals, fruit or vegetable juices, and fresh fruits and vegetables. The program requires that vouchers (or food packages) be tailored (by food type and amount) by category of recipient—e.g., infants, children; pregnant, postpartum and nursing mothers. In addition to food benefits, recipients also must receive nutrition education and breast-feeding support (where called for) and may receive other services like referral to medical care providers.

The federal cost of providing WIC benefits varies widely depending on the recipient and the foods prescribed in recipients' vouchers, as well as differences in retail prices (vouchers are denominated in food amounts, not dollars) and administrative and nutrition services expenses (like those for nutrition risk screening, breastfeeding support, and nutrition education). Moreover, the program's food costs are significantly influenced by the degree to which states gain rebates from infant formula (and, in some cases, juice or other) manufacturers under a requirement to pursue "cost containment" strategies; these rebates recently have totaled to over $1.8 billion a year nationwide and pay for the cost of serving a significant portion of the WIC population. In FY2007, the national average federal cost of a WIC food package (after rebates) was $39 a month for each participant. The program also provides states with funding for administrative costs and nutrition services (like nutrition education). In FY2007, the average monthly "nutrition services and administrative" ("NSA") cost, including regular administrative expenses and nutrition risk assessments and nutrition education, was about $16 per case.

The WIC Program has categorical, income, and nutrition risk requirements for eligibility. Only pregnant and postpartum women, infants, and children under age 5 may participate. As noted above, WIC applicants must show evidence of health or nutrition risk, medically verified by a health professional, in order to qualify. They also must have family income below 185% of the most recent annually indexed federal poverty guidelines ($32,560 a year for a three person family for the period July 2008-June 2009; state WIC agencies may (but virtually never) set lower income eligibility cutoff points. Receipt of TANF, SNAP benefits (formerly, food stamps), or Medicaid assistance also can satisfy the WIC Program's income test, and states may consider pregnant women meeting the income test “presumptively” eligible until a nutritional risk evaluation is made. In 2006, 60% of WIC enrollees had family income below the federal poverty guidelines, 9% of WIC enrollees were cash welfare (TANF) recipients, 22% received food stamps, and 63% were covered by Medicaid.

WIC participants receive benefits for a specified period of time, and in some cases must be recertified during this period to show continuing need—e.g., pregnant women may continue to receive benefits throughout their pregnancy and for up to 6-12 months after childbirth. Although it is federally funded, the WIC program actually is administered by some 2,000 state and local health agencies (and more than 30 Indian tribal organizations participating as separate grantees and treated like states). Over 10,000 local clinics/sites carry out the program. State administrative responsibilities extend to certifying eligibility, distributing benefits, issuing benefits, redeeming vouchers, and approving retail stores for participation.

Unlike most other federal nutrition assistance programs, the WIC program is not an “entitlement” program; it is “discretionary” and participation and benefits are limited by the amount of federal funding appropriated, whatever state supplementary funding is provided, and the extent of manufacturers' rebates.

However, Congress has historically provided funding at levels that meet participation and food cost requirements—so-called “full funding.” In FY2007, federal spending was $5.4 billion, and the program served a monthly average of 8.3 million women, infants, and children: 25% women, 27% infants, and 51% children. In addition to the regular WIC program (which includes special vouchers for fruits and vegetables), annual Agriculture Department appropriations (in a budget account separate from WIC appropriations) fund a small ($20 million a year) WIC farmers’ market nutrition program under which WIC applicants and recipients receive additional vouchers for the purchase of fresh produce at farmers’ markets. Table 3 summarizes WIC participation and federal spending.

Spending is made up of food costs, just over 70% of the total in recent years, and nutrition services and administrative (NSA) expenses (of which approximately two-thirds are typically for service activities like nutrition education and nutrition risk evaluations and one-third is for traditional administrative activities like eligibility determinations and issuing and redeeming vouchers).

Table 3. Special Supplemental Nutrition Program for Women, Infants, and Children (WIC) Participation and Federal Spending for Selected Fiscal Years, 1980-2007 In Millions

	Average monthly participation				Federal spending	
	Women	Infants	Children	Total[a]	Current dollars[b]	Constant 2007 dollars[c]
1980	0.4	0.5	1.0	1.9	$727.7	$1,867.3
1985	0.6	0.9	1.6	3.1	1,489.3	2,866.9
1990	1.0	1.4	2.1	4.5	2,122.4	3,385.2
1995	1.6	1.8	3.5	6.9	3,436.2	4,659.5
1996	1.6	1.8	3.7	7.2	2,301.1	3,035.1
1997	1.7	1.9	3.8	7.4	3,843.8	4,939.3
1998	1.7	1.9	3.7	7.3	3,890.4	4,917.5
1999	1.7	1.9	3.7	7.3	3,938.1	4,883.2
2000	1.8	1.9	3.5	7.2	3,982.1	4,786.6
2001	1.8	1.9	3.6	7.3	4,153.3	4,838.6
2002	1.8	1.9	3.8	7.5	4,339.8	4,982.1
2003	1.9	1.9	3.8	7.6	4,524.4	5,071.9
2004	1.9	2.0	4.0	7.9	4,887.3	5,356.5
2005	2.0	2.0	4.0	8.0	4,993.1	5,297.7
2006	2.0	2.1	4.0	8.1	5,075.7	5,192.4
2007	2.1	2.2	4.0	8.3	5,417.9	5,417.9

Source: Compiled by the Congressional Research Service (CRS) based on data from the U.S. Department of Agriculture, Food and Nutrition Service.

a. Details may not sum to totals due to rounding.

b. Includes funding for food costs, administration, nutrition services, studies, surveys, pilots, and farmers' market programs. Does not include support from manufacturer rebates for infant formula and juices.

c. Constant dollars were calculated using the fiscal year CPI-U.

DAY CARE, SUMMER, AND AFTER-SCHOOL PROGRAMS

In addition to the school-day-based lunch and breakfast programs, child nutrition laws include provisions for federal subsidies and commodity support for schools and other institutions/ organizations offering meals and snacks to children in outside-of-school program settings. This assistance is provided to (1) schools and other governmental institutions, (2) private for-profit and nonprofit day care centers, (3) family/group day care homes, and (4) nongovernmental institutions/organizations that offer outside-of-school programs for children. In addition, day care centers for chronically impaired adults and elderly persons are eligible for assistance under the same general terms as centers caring for children.

Federal support for day care, summer, and outside-of-school meal/snack programs totaled some $2.5 billion in "entitlement" funding (including a small amount of commodities) for FY2007. More than 5 million children (and 100,000 adults) participated.

Child and Adult Care Food Program (CACFP)

The large majority of assistance for meals and snacks served in outside-of-school settings is provided under the CACFP. This program pays subsidies for meals and snacks served in participating nonresidential child care centers (average attendance 40-5 0 children) and family day care homes (typically caring for 5-10 children). It also supports assistance for meals and snacks in adult day care centers (averaging 40-45 chronically ill or elderly adults), as well as those offered in participating after-school programs (which are discussed later).

The CACFP provides federal payments for breakfasts, lunches, suppers, and snacks served in participating centers or homes. In many cases, sponsors giving administrative support to providers also are paid limited amounts for their costs. Subsidized meals and snacks must meet minimum federal nutrition standards, and providers must fulfill any state or local licensing/approval requirements or minimum alternative federal requirements (or otherwise demonstrate that they comply with government established standards for other child care programs). Federal assistance is made up overwhelmingly of cash subsidies based on the number of meals/snacks served and federally set indexed per-meal/snack subsidy rates; about 3% is in the form of federally donated food commodities. CACFP subsidies are available for meals and snacks served to children age 12 or under, migrant children age 15 or under, handicapped children of any age, and (in the case of adult care centers) chronically impaired and elderly adults; but preschool children form the overwhelming majority of those served by the program. Federal CACFP payments flow to individual providers either directly from the administering state agency (this is the case with many child/adult care centers able to handle their own administrative responsibilities) or through "sponsors" who oversee and provide support for a number of local providers (this is the case with some child/adult care centers and all day care homes).

Child care centers in the CACFP can be: (1) public or private nonprofit centers, (2) Head Start centers, (3) for-profit proprietary centers (if they meet minimum requirements as to the proportion of low-income children they enroll), and (4) shelters for homeless families. Adult day care centers include public or private nonprofit centers and for-profit proprietary centers (if they meet minimum requirements related to serving low-income disabled and elderly adults). In FY2007, some 48,000 child care centers, with average daily attendance of 2.2 million children, participated in the CACFP. Adult care centers totaled 2,500, with an average daily attendance of 105,000 persons.

Participating day care centers may receive daily subsidies for up to two meals and one snack or one meal and two snacks for each child, so long as they meet federal nutrition standards. All meals and snacks served in centers are federally subsidized to at least some degree; different subsidies are provided for breakfasts, lunches/suppers, and snacks, and subsidy rates are set in law and indexed for inflation annually. However, cash subsidies vary according to the family income of each child's family, and the income demographics of the centers' recipients is periodically evaluated. Subsidies are annually indexed, and the largest subsidies are paid for meals and snacks served to children with family income below 130% of the federal poverty income guidelines (the income limit for free school meals): for July 2008-June 2009, these subsidies are 71 cents for each snack, $1.40 for each breakfast, and $2.57 for each lunch/supper. Smaller subsidies are available for meals and snacks served at a reduced price (no more than 15 cents for snacks, 30 cents for breakfasts, and 40 cents for lunches/suppers) to children with family income between 130% and 185% of the poverty guidelines (the income range for reduced-price school meals) and for meals and snacks served to children who do not qualify for free or reduced- price meals/snacks. "Independent" centers (those without sponsors handling administrative responsibilities) must pay for administrative costs associated with the CACFP out of non-federal funds or a portion of their meal subsidy payments. In other cases, center sponsors may retain a proportion of the meal subsidy payments they receive on behalf of their centers to cover their costs. Finally, federal commodity assistance is available to centers, valued at some 21 cents a meal for July 2008-June 2009 (the same commodity value provided for school meals).

CACFP subsidized day care homes serve an average of 5-10 children; just under 30% of children in the CACFP (860,000 in FY2007) are served through day care homes, and about one-third of the money spent under the CACFP supports meals and snacks served in homes. In FY2007, 143,000 home sites (with some 900 sponsors) received subsidies.

As with centers, payments to day care homes are provided for no more than two meals and one snack (or one meal and two snacks) a day for each child. Unlike centers, day care homes must participate under the auspices of a public or (most often) private nonprofit sponsor that typically has 100 or more homes under its supervision; CACFP day care home sponsors receive monthly administrative payments (separate from meal subsidies) based on the number of homes for which they are responsible. Also unlike centers, day care homes receive cash subsidies (but not commodities) that generally do not differ by individual children's family income. Instead, there are two distinct, annually indexed subsidy rates. "Tier I" homes (those located in low-income areas or operated by low income providers) receive higher subsidies for each meal/snack they serve: for July 2008-June 2009, all lunches and suppers are subsidized at \$2.18 each, all breakfasts at \$1.17, and all snacks at 65 cents. "Tier II" homes (those not located in low-income areas or without low income providers) receive smaller subsidies: for July 2008-June 2009, these are \$1.31 for lunches/suppers, 43 cents for breakfasts, and 18 cents for snacks. However, Tier II providers may seek the higher Tier I subsidy rates for individual low income children for whom financial information is collected and verified.

Although federal subsidies for day care centers differ by family income, there is no requirement that meals/snacks specifically identified as "free" or "reduced-price" be served. Centers may adjust their regular fees (tuition) to account for federal payments, but the CACFP itself does not regulate these fees; in addition, centers can charge separately for meals/snacks, so long as there are no charges for children meeting free-meal/snack income tests and limited charges for those meeting reduced-price income tests. Federal subsidies for family day care homes differ by the type of home and homes may adjust their tuition to account for federal payments; as with centers, there is no requirement that meals/snacks specifically identified as "free" or "reduced-price" be offered. However, unlike centers, federal rules prohibit any separate meal charges.

In FY2007, the CACFP provided $2.1 billion in cash subsidies for meal costs and $77 million worth of commodities. In addition, it paid $137 million for sponsors' administrative costs and expenses related to auditing local operators.

Summer Food Service Program

The Summer Food Service program provides assistance to local public and private nonprofit "service institutions" running summer youth/recreation programs, summer feeding projects, and camps. Assistance is primarily in the form of cash subsidies for each meal or snack served; however, federally donated commodities also are offered. Participating service institutions (also called sponsors) often, but not of necessity, are entities that provide ongoing year-round service to the community and include schools, local governments, camps, colleges and universities in the National Youth Sports program, and private nonprofit organizations like churches.

Sponsors of three types of summer programs can be approved: (1) "open" sites operating in lower-income areas where 50% or more of the children have family income that would make them eligible for free or reduced-price school meals, (2) "enrolled" sites where at least half of the children enrolled in the sponsor's program are eligible for free or reduced-price school meals, and (3) summer camps. Summer meals/snacks are provided free to all children at open or enrolled sites and to lower-income children in camps.

Summer sponsors get operating (food, storage, labor) cost subsidies for all meals/snacks they serve—one meal and one snack, or two meals (three meals for children in programs for migrant children) per child per day. In addition, sponsors receive payments for administrative costs, and states are provided with subsidies for administrative costs and health and meal-quality inspections. For the summer of 2008, the combined (operating and administrative cost) subsidies under the summer program were approximately $3 for each lunch/supper, $1.70 for each breakfast, and 70 cents for each snack. Actual payments vary slightly (e.g., by about 5 cents for lunches) depending on the location of the site (e.g., rural vs. urban) and whether meals are prepared on-site or by a vendor.

In FY2007, some 3,600 sponsors (with 30,000 food service sites) participated in the summer program and served an average of 1.9 million children daily. Program costs totaled to about $300 million, including cash, commodities, administrative cost assistance, and health inspection costs.

After-School Programs

Federal assistance for snacks (and, in some cases, meals) served through after-school programs is provided through two basic alternatives. The CACFP offers subsidies to sponsors (schools or community-based nonprofit sponsoring entities) for snacks served during the school year to "at- risk" children in after-school programs located in lower-income areas where at least half the children are eligible for free or reduced-price school meals. In a few states (eight in FY2009), these CACFP payments also are available for meals (typically suppers) through after-school programs. All snacks/meals generally are served free. A second, less-used, avenue is open only to schools as an extension of the School Lunch program. They may operate after-school snack-only programs during the school year that provide free snacks in lower-income areas (like the CACFP component) or offer free, reduced-price, or fully paid-for snacks (differentiated by family income like the School Lunch program) in non-needy areas.

Although non-school sponsors may receive after-school nutrition assistance, the overwhelming majority of sites (more than 80%) are operated by schools. Federal cash subsidies for snacks (and, where available, meals) generally are the same as those paid for snacks and lunches/suppers in the regular CACFP. In FY2007, average daily participation in after-school snack/supper programs was approximately 1.2 million children. Spending on this type of assistance is not separately tracked at the federal level, but is included in the figures for the School Lunch program and the CACFP, noted above.

Other Child Nutrition Programs, Initiatives, and Support Activities

Child nutrition laws also support a range of smaller programs, initiatives, and activities.

States are entitled to federal grants to help cover administrative and oversight/monitoring costs associated with child nutrition programs. The national amount each year is equal to about 1.5% of child nutrition cash support. The majority of this money is allocated to states based on their share of spending on the covered programs; about 15% is allocated under a discretionary formula granting each state additional amounts for the CACFP, commodity distribution, and "coordinated review" efforts. In addition, states receive payments for their role in overseeing summer programs (about 2.5% of their summer program aid). States are free to apportion their federal administrative expense payments among child nutrition initiatives (including commodity distribution activities) as they see fit. State administrative expense funding in FY2007 totaled to more than $160 million.

States receive grants for a Fresh Fruit and Vegetable program, under which selected schools in each state get money to purchase and distribute fresh fruits and vegetables to all children in attendance (regardless of family income). Money is distributed by a formula under which about half the funding is distributed equally to each state and the remainder is allocated by state population; states select participating schools (with an emphasis on those with a higher proportion of low-income children) and set annual per student grant amounts (between $50 and $75). Funding is set by law at $40 million for the 2008-2009 school year, $65 million for the 2009- 2010 school year, $101 million for the 2010-2011 school year, $150 million for the 2011-2012 school year, and inflation-indexed for later years.

Schools and institutions like summer camps and child care facilities not otherwise participating in federally subsidized meal service programs, along with schools with split (part-day) sessions for kindergartners or pre-kindergartners where children do not have access to regular school meal programs, can participate in the Special Milk program. Under this program, they provide milk to all children at a reduced-price or free. Each half-pint served is federally subsidized at a slightly different rate, depending on whether it is served free or not, but the provision of free milk to needy children is not required. In FY2007, about 90 million half-pints were subsidized at about 15 cents each (7% were served free) to roughly 500,000 children. Federal costs for this program typically run about $15 million a year.

Under a coordinated review effort (CRE), the FNS, in cooperation with state agencies, conducts periodic school compliance and accountability evaluations to improve management and identify administrative, subsidy claim, and meal quality problems. This $5 million-a-year effort is the major ongoing initiative related to maintaining the integrity of child nutrition programs. The Agriculture Department's Economic Research Service (ERS) and the FNS conduct nutrition research, studies, surveys, and program evaluations (typically totaling about $10 million a year). A national Food Service Management Institute (FSMI) provides technical assistance, instruction, and materials related to nutrition and food service management; it is funded at $4 million a year. An information clearinghouse provides information to support community sponsored food assistance initiatives, using funding of about $250,000 a year. Special FNS projects – "Team Nutrition" nutrition education initiatives, a food safety project, technical assistance to program operators, food service training grants, aid with electronic food resource systems, "program integrity" efforts – are aimed at helping schools and other providers with nutrition education materials, assisting them to improve their meal service operations and the quality of meals, and ensuring that federal support is spent correctly; they are typically funded at $15-$20 million a year.

INDEX

G

H

I

J

K

L

M

N

O

P

Q

R

V

W